HOLY DYING

Stories and Struggles

HOLY DYING

Stories and Struggles

Ellen Richardson

Church Publishing
NEW YORK

Unless otherwise noted, the Scripture quotations contained herein are from the New Revised Standard Version Bible, copyright © 1989 by the Division of Christian Education of the National Council of Churches of Christ in the U.S.A. Used by permission. All rights reserved.

Scripture quotations from the book of Psalms, unless otherwise indicated, are from the Book of Common Prayer (New York: Church Publishing, 1979).

Church Publishing
19 East 34th Street
New York, NY 10016
www.churchpublishing.org

Cover design by Jennifer Kopec, 2Pug Design
Typeset by Rose Design

Library of Congress Cataloging-in-Publication Data

Names: Richardson, Ellen (Episcopal Priest), author.
Title: Holy dying : stories and struggles / Ellen Richardson.
Description: New York : Church Publishing, 2017.
Identifiers: LCCN 2016045046 (print) | LCCN 2017001772 (ebook) | ISBN 9780819233363 (pbk.) | ISBN 9780819233370 (ebook)
Subjects: LCSH: Death—Religious aspects—Christianity. | Episcopal Church—Doctrines.
Classification: LCC BT825 .R485 2017 (print) | LCC BT825 (ebook) | DDC 236/.1—dc23
LC record available at https://lccn.loc.gov/2016045046

Printed in Canada

FOR MARK

For we know that if the earthly tent we live in is destroyed, we have a building from God, a house not made with hands, eternal in the heavens. For in this tent we groan, longing to be clothed with our heavenly dwelling—if indeed, when we have taken it off we will not be found naked. For while we are still in this tent, we groan under our burden, because we wish not to be unclothed but to be further clothed, so that what is mortal may be swallowed up by life. He who has prepared us for this very thing is God, who has given us the Spirit as a guarantee.

—2 Corinthians 5:1–5

CONTENTS

Hospice Stories

Do you work wonders for the dead?
  Will those who have died stand up and give
    you thanks?
Will your loving-kindness be declared in the grave?
  Your faithfulness in the land of destruction?
Will your wonders be known in the dark?
  Or your righteousness in the country where all
    is forgotten?
                                —PSALM 88:11–13 BCP

I am not sure what made you pick up or order or download this book, but I have a pretty good idea. Someone you know and love is seriously ill and expected to die soon, or already has. Or someone you care about is caring for a family member struggling with a worsening chronic or life-threatening illness. Or you yourself are anticipating being the one cared for. Or you have somehow survived a caregiving experience and are, as you grieve, trying to process what it was all about. Perhaps you are a professional health caregiver or pastor who spends your work life offering your gifts and your skills to the support of others, and are curious to find new or helpful insight here, some story that might affirm your calling or ease the burden of your compassion fatigue. I hope some of you are reading this book with a supportive group of friends, in a book group or Sunday school class, and that it provides plenty for you to chew on—together. I hope there is something for each of you here in my stories.

I am a physician who loved my years of work in family practice in small-town America and its metamorphosis to years of work in the medical specialty of hospice and palliative care in larger towns and metro suburban/rural areas.

I am also an Episcopal priest. My bi-vocational perspective as both doctor and pastor has affected my work with patients and families in medical settings and in Christian communities of faith. Initially I saw this call to walk simultaneously in the worlds of medicine and theology as one of healing by creating bridges between them; perhaps that was too ambitious, or too naive. Now having retired from the practice of medicine, I work full time in the church with a focus on pastoral care. Patients are now parishioners, but their experience of suffering from the impact of serious progressive illness and impending death does not change with my professional perspective.

Years ago, and not long after I had traded in my small town primary care practice to begin working full time in hospice and palliative care, I found myself testifying before lights and cameras in a somewhat intimidating committee meeting of the Georgia General Assembly. I was speaking in favor of a bill that would release a legal restriction on hospice corporations from caring exclusively for patients with a prognosis of less than six months. The intention was to open up the possibility for hospice companies in Georgia to offer their well-trained professional staff to provide palliative care in hospital settings for patients who had a prognosis longer than six months and were receiving ongoing disease-directed treatments, and who often desperately needed expert management of pain and other distressing symptoms. As I was trying to explain to the committee the continuum of palliative care and hospice care and the interdisciplinary holistic approach that included social, emotional, psychological, and spiritual support, I was interrupted by a representative in the back row who said in a deep Southern accent, "Little lady, aren't you a doctor?"

"Yes sir," I responded.

He looked displeased and said, "Then what gives you the *authority* (his emphasis) to comment on *spiritual* matters?"

Well, he had me there, as this occurred very early in my process of formal discernment for holy orders in the Episcopal Church, and I did not have the theological credentials at the time to respond with the integrity he was looking for. Had I not been raised in Georgia I might have taken offense at his derision and lost my manners. Yet this gentleman was merely expressing our cultural dualism and the boundaries that we imprint upon ourselves, parsing the suffering body to the doctor, and the suffering spirit to the pastor. I know that this particular Georgia legislator believed that each sphere has its own proper authority, and for a long time he had me convinced, too.

I had always seen my job as a physician as one of engagement in listening and observation, discerning and diagnosing, and then finding and offering a solution to a particular problem or set of problems brought to me by a patient. I have come to see my job as a priest in much the same way: listening and observing, discerning and praying, and then searching for some hopefully helpful perspective on the problems brought to me by those seeking guidance. Not very different, really, except for the praying part.

I have always respected and protected those boundaries of body, mind, and spirit both as a physician and as a priest, insofar as they have been constructed by any one person to maintain personal privacy and safety. For the most part, parishioners have generally avoided asking me medical advice, and have found that when they did, I was loath to give it, instead encouraging them to see their own physicians. Patients whom I visited as a hospice physician did not, with notable exceptions, seek my spiritual counsel, and I offered my presence during prayer only when specifically invited by a patient or family to do so. The origin of this deep respect for personal boundaries of body, mind, and spirit can be traced, in part, to the cultural adoption of a phrase from Thomas Jefferson: "a wall of separation between church and state." This concept, applicable to *public* governance, has over time become imbedded into a concept of *personal governance*,[1] which affects how we live, how we deal with illness, and how we die.

As we treat our bodies and spirits as separate creatures inhabiting the same space, a Greek idea that became foundational in early Christian theology, we are at risk for a personal disintegration when confronted with serious illness, trauma, and dying. When overcome by life-threatening illness and its weakness and decline, acutely focused on the failures of the body, we find ourselves isolated from the faith communities that tend our souls—unable to attend worship as we once did, unable to participate in the ministries to and with others that once gave great meaning to our lives. Our physical selves are given over to the world of medicine and science as our spiritual selves are rendered to the Sunday bulletin prayer list or the parish online prayer chain and brief, awkward visits, embarrassed by our vulnerability

---

1. Jefferson's letter to the Danbury Baptists, from the digital collection of the Library of Congress, *http://www.loc.gov/loc/lcib/9806/danpre.html*.

and loss of autonomy and function. We have lost a communal integrating language to address our decline other than in prayers that may beg God's mercy to heal, hoping for a reversal or erasure of our current physical circumstances, for a restoration to what was before, for a turning back to a time before we knew suffering. Our prayers of anger, abandonment, despair, remorse, and desperation become cries in the isolation of the night. Well-meaning others keep a distance from our pain, valuing privacy and safety over the danger of contagion in a shared suffering. Each of us winds up alone, with a few family members or a close friend if we are blessed; this means that each story of dying is written as if it were the first story of its kind. We have not witnessed the dying time of others; others are kept at a distance from ours. We are therefore left to wrestle with all of our questions about suffering and dying alone, as if no one had ever gotten sick or died before, as if the questions had never been asked before, as if others had never struggled with the answers before.

This book is about these medical, physical, emotional, and spiritual questions: how to ask them, how to wrestle with them, and what good might come out of this wrestling match. How does the faithful Christian love life, savor life, choose life, honor the sacredness of life created in God's image, and still stay ready to honor life's limits, its very temporary nature, its passing? How can anyone know and trust when medicine has done all it can to sustain a particular life, and when it should step back from prolonging a particular death? How do we accept responsibility and approach repentance for illnesses that arise from a long history of self-abuse and neglect of our own bodies; how much can we expect the world of medicine (and God) to save us from the consequences of self-destruction? How are some people able to face impending death with acceptance and peace, reconciling a lifetime of broken health and relationships, while others, even those who profess or proclaim faith in the ways of God and God's promise of an everlasting life, fight death with every fiber of their being—even in the setting of immense physical and emotional suffering? Why is this fight accepted as noble and heroic in our wider culture, and surrender to a peaceful death called "giving up"? What does it mean when family members demand prolonged and non-purposeful technologies for a dying person because a loved one's time is "in God's hands"? Where do family caregivers find the guidance, acceptance, and peace to release the beloved from these death-prolonging and death-avoiding treatments and find the trust to let them go to God?

These questions, and many like them, have been my daily fare, and the daily fare of many who are called to work with patients and families approaching the last phase of a life. Over my time in hospice and palliative care, neither the questions nor the answers became any easier. The intellectual understanding that everyone and every living thing dies (eventually) seems to have no bearing on personal choices, for even in the twenty-first century most people are apprehensive to make the sacred space necessary to talk about dying. There is so much fear surrounding even speaking of death that misguided politicians have called attempts to create opportunities in health care settings for such conversation "death panels," as if just *talking* about thoughts and feelings about life's final days is tantamount to killing. With so little support for the topic, doctors avoid it, and patients and their families allow this, resisting and avoiding any talk that would "destroy hope." Pastors are tempted to capitulate to the wider culture, as the very ill and dying and those who care for them often invite pastoral support only within the language of miracle and the power of prayer to cure illnesses and sustain life. The powerful message of the death-conquering Overcoming One and the Resurrection is saved for the funeral. The pastor may be expected to stay silent or to challenge the medical team who is "giving up hope," and to challenge the family not to "lose faith" while all are gathered in the ICU waiting room. What if there were an equal expectation for the pastor to challenge the family by asking what part of insisting on indefinite, limitless, resource-intensive, full life support for a body experiencing multi-organ system failure is "choosing life"? Where is the church in these needed conversations?

This book comes from my place along a much longer journey that each of us must take toward healing and wholeness. Part story, part memoir, part theological reflection, and part soapbox, it is about medical *and* spiritual matters, looking for an interface of understanding and compassion in places of fear and sorrow. I could say I have chosen these stories from the thousands I have lived as a doctor and a pastor that left me with clarity of memory or meaning, but mostly they have chosen me. That the stories' details of time and space, relationships and names have been shifted enough to protect privacy does not diminish their essence, nor their power to teach, to question, to challenge, and to reveal a way in the wilderness and rivers in the desert. My prayer is that these stories, and the questions they generate, give you pause, disturb you enough to ask more questions, and bring you strength for your journey.

CHAPTER 1

Harder Days

> They did not ask, "Where is the LORD, who brought us up out of Egypt and led us through the barren wilderness, through a land of deserts and ravines, a land of drought and utter darkness, a land where no one travels and no one lives?"
>
> —JEREMIAH 2:6

Several years into what I thought would be a lifetime career as a rural family physician, I came to believe that much of what was brought into my homey solo practice and laid into my lap over the years was a kind of suffering for which I did not have a ready balm. There was physical illness to be managed to be sure, and I tried to offer advice and guidance to help my patients stay as healthy as possible in the face of burdensome illness. Most of my energy, however, was consumed by trying to care for problems of a more challenging sort. The joyful office days were filled with well babies, routine check-ups, medication refill visits, mild contagious diseases that got better, and good catch-up conversations usually about hunting, fishing, upcoming holidays, or grandchildren. The harder days were marked by a pervasive sense of brokenness: patients who could not manage to take their medications, check their blood sugars, get any sleep, leave abusive relationships, stop smoking, or even attempt to exercise. Their chronic conditions provided the diagnosis code for their visits, but it was the headaches, the back pain, the chronic coughing, and the indigestion that brought them in. The underbelly of the presenting symptoms was lined with grief, sorrow, loneliness, depression, marital and family discord and dysfunction, alcohol or drug addiction, troubled children or grandchildren, difficulty on the job or unemployment and financial distress, or just the mounting weight of being overwhelmed with life as they knew it.

I could offer a medical test, a prescription, a referral to a medical specialist or a counselor, and a sympathetic ear—mostly they came in to be listened to. I began to see that all my sincere offers of insight, context, and perspective fell short of the mark, and that I was not really able to help in any fundamental way; I could not make them better. Opportunities to explore root causes of psychosocial distress were generally declined in favor of a search for root causes of physical illness, so instead of being able to offer healing, I offered blood tests, CAT scans, prescriptions, and referrals. The search for a "real" diagnosis, the identification of the precise place where the body had failed, became the focus of attention. With due diligence I used all my powers of knowledge and experience to find a disease, to give it a name, and to access every means, therapeutic, pharmacologic, or technologic, to eliminate it. Still, most of the time, I could not make them better, if better meant wholeness of body, mind, and spirit.

And then, some of them got *really* sick. Sometimes it was that chronic condition suffering for lack of attention that got away from them. The high blood pressure became the heart failure became the kidney failure or stroke. Sometimes it was the unexpected "out of the blue" rare disease—usually cancer—that rocked their worlds in that "I never thought it would happen to me" way. The nature of the threat would call for a specialist; I would refer the patient, and then be relegated to the side wings of the stage while a stronger magic was sought for and delivered by "experts" whose authority and credibility increased with the geographical distance from my small town. Patients whom I had considered "mine," in my small primary care practice, belonged for a time to the specialist(s), and while they suffered every effort to prolong their lives threatened by terminal disease, I waited for them to come home.

Usually they did come home, and some of them taught me something remarkable about dying that I had never learned in medical school or training. When all medicines and treatments had run their course and were exhausted, when patients were often the most uncomfortable, the most weak, the most anxious, and the least able to maintain their defenses, an unbidden grace would surface, creating openings in their lives and relationships, making room for repentance and forgiveness, and for healing— even as their bodies were failing.

Where did that grace come from, and what was it about the project of facing death that called it forth? Which people paid attention to that grace and which ones denied and declined it? What was it that allowed some people facing their final weeks and days to finally see what was important in their lives and to attend to their unfinished business? What kept others from this path that seemed to lead to a spiritual peace in the setting of a failing body? What was I missing in all my efforts to "doctor" my patients? I wanted to harness this healing power and offer it to everyone who was struggling, as if I could write prescriptions for grace, repentance, or forgiveness.

My identity as a physician slowly evolved through the many stories in my career from one of director of the production, as I believed myself trained to be, to one of witness and companion to those who suffered. I suppose this shift in identity smoothed the way to the eventual transition from doctor to priest. At first this was uncomfortable, and encompassed an acknowledgement of failure to really fix things, for I was long and dutifully and expensively educated for many years of my life to do just that— fix things. Over time and experience, especially with dying patients, I saw that "fixing" role begin to unravel; I stepped back for a wider view, and began to un-learn what I thought I knew about healing.

One of my earliest teachers was Robert; he was my first-ever hospice patient. A transplant to the Deep South, a child-follower who after retirement moved from Chicago to live with his daughter and the sweet Southern boy she married. Robert was intelligent and feisty, thin and polished and a fish out of water, but the family bond was strong and Robert's daughter and son-in-law brought him into their home.

Robert had a delightful talent with skills he had honed over years of his life. He created tiny panoramas inside eggshells— whole miniature worlds inside eggs of all sizes from every imaginable species of bird or fowl that had laid them. Every one I saw was an exquisite work of unimaginable patience and skill; some of them even included tiny artificial lights inside the finished tableaus, running off of tiny batteries. These were no seasonal bunny cutouts in sugared shells; these were works of art and craft like I have never seen since, except in a museum.

Robert had enjoyed his retirement and practicing his art in his daughter's home, which had been remodeled to provide a studio filled with stacks of tiny drawers filled with the miniscule objects he placed inside the eggs and around the edges of their openings. He was a gracious person and was generous in show-ing off his treasures and works-in-progress. He had been blessed with good health and had stayed active and trim for much of his life, most of which was spent working in automobile man-ufacturing plants in Michigan. When he began to develop symptoms that lead to a diagnosis of a stage IV cancer with a prognosis of less than six months, I would have expected one so committed to the smallest details of his art to have researched and attacked his cancer with the same diligence. I would have expected him to find a specialist to guide his pilgrimage towards healing himself of this intrusive and objectionable interruption in his life, just when he was beginning to really enjoy retirement and make new friends.

Robert did approach his cancer with attention to details, but without the shock and subsequent emotional desperation that was familiar to me. He kept himself aware of his disease pro-gression, was particular about his symptom management, and would only accept disease-directed treatment that had great odds of helping him, and small odds of making him miserable; he said yes to radiation, and no to chemotherapy, which in his case had little chance of offering him extended time with the quality of life that he wanted. Instead, Robert concentrated on who and what he loved and conserved his energy for his art. He got his affairs in order, talked openly about dying, and became a pioneer patient in a small south Georgia town for a new med-ical service called hospice. He went about bringing to life those ideas still in his imagination—unfinished work in eggshells of every size and shade of ivory that sat still in their pristine forms, like blank canvases cushioned in straw. He worked in his studio every day, until he was too weak from his illness to sit up for long. When he began the dying phase of his illness, he was calm, at peace, and full of gratitude for his life.

I do not remember Robert using language that was particularly religious; I doubt if he ever used the word "healing," and yet he saw his life as part of a greater context in which he was only a part, and not the central fulcrum. I do not remember any stories he might have told about his life before I knew him, though I am sure he carried as many stories as most of us. He did look forward to reuniting after his death with people he had loved who had died before him—his wife, and a brother. I do remember that he did not seem to be afraid of dying, something that was rare at that time in my professional life and experience.

Robert, and many who came after him, taught me that healing was not something I was to conjure up and present to my patients, but something that comes from within each person. Healing is not rendered in the pursuit of the diagnosis, or the treatment of it, as my doctor brain had been trained to believe. Healing comes from the heart of one who is open to believing in something greater than self, one who sees the cycle of human life as part of a greater whole, one who believes in "a God who is merciful and gracious, slow to anger, and abounding in steadfast love and faithfulness" (Exodus 34:6). As I have grown in my understanding and authenticity to speak of spiritual matters, I have come to believe that healing is the breath of God that falls on each of us, just as the sun and the rain. It is a mercy that is not wanton or wasteful, but waits for each of us to recognize its presence when we need it most, on those harder days when hopelessness and brokenness seem to be the order of the day. This healing is that thing we are all looking for and do not know it. It is that thing that makes the difference—not between living and dying, but between dying in stress and anxiety and dying in peace.

How can we recognize healing in ourselves and in others? Is healing something that we can promote or just recognize and accept? Does it require specific requests in prayer? How can we embrace an understanding of healing that is deeper and more powerful than just restoration to a life without illness or brokenness?

CHAPTER 2

Take Me Home to Die

The sparrow has found her a house
and the swallow a nest where she may lay her young;
    by the side of your altars, O Lord of hosts,
    my King and my God.
                    —Psalm 84:2 BCP

Much of the life of a small town doctor is like any other life: a balance of home and work, schedules and schedule adjustments, routine and crisis, frustrations and satisfactions, and relationships, both professional and personal, most of which are connected to other relationships. In my solo family practice the wonderful people who ran my office knew everyone in our town, who they were married to or related to, and sometimes who they *used to be* married to, and this gave me not only a needed heads-up with my own patients, but a deeper appreciation for how complexly woven any one life could be. It was my great joy to care for newborn infants and great grandmothers, siblings in preschool and siblings who were grandparents themselves. Family was a concept that extended far into the community, encompassing partners, neighbors, long time coworkers, church members, in-laws from long-dissolved marriages, and assorted indefinable relationships—from the previously estranged offspring to the long-term paid household helper evolving into compassionate caregiver.

I had always made home visits to see patients since first introduced to the idea in family practice training. Unfortunately this practice of visiting patients at home has become rare, as the constraints of time and economy do not make home visits practical. It is also understandable that some people might decline home visits for reasons of privacy. However, for someone ill and unable to be transported by caregivers to a clinic or office setting for non-emergency care, a home visit was a convenience to the patient, and in most cases a great blessing of hospitality to me. These visits on the patient's turf are naturally more patient- and family-focused than can be accomplished on "health care" turf. They can involve family pets, curious toddlers, and almost universally the competition of the television playing in the background. At home, it is easier to see caregiving challenges, including the physical barriers to safe care that might be overcome with options outside of the family's imagination, or that might not have been mentioned in the office visit, for fear of making the patient feel a burden on her family. A home visit is also a more open window into the person who is distilled in the medical office to "an appointment," expediently represented by a chart of medical history and lab values. At home, the old photographs on display, the handmade quilt on the bed that was handed down from a great-grandmother, the flower garden and bird-feeders outside the window, the offer of a cup of tea, all become gifts to be opened to a deeper understanding of who it is that needs care, and how that care can best be offered. I have visited homes where I was expected to remove my shoes at the door, and had a sense that I was contaminating a pristine environment; I have been in homes where I quickly sized up whether it might be safe to sit down on furniture that looked salvaged from the side of the road. Mostly, I was welcomed, and honored to be invited in.

Home is a concept with profound cultural and religious significance throughout the ages; the place where we take our rest from the world, where we prepare, eat, and even grow our meals, where we keep our stuff, and when asked, where the majority of Americans would choose to die.[1] Home can be a quiet sanctuary, or a loud, crowded multi-generational, multi-language dwelling full of siblings, cousins, babies, animals, and elders. Depending on our social and economic privilege or our cultural orientation, home can be a place of permanency and identity, or a series of spaces we take on and discard along a grander plan of work or progressive prosperity. To an immigrant family, home can be two rooms in the basement of a distant relative or acquaintance. To the elderly who can no longer care for themselves, home can be the space between a hospital bed in a shared room and a wheelchair in the hall. To the homeless, home can be something irretrievably lost. Our history, experience, and memories of home have much to do with how we think about being home in this world, and how we think about our hope for an eternal home with God.

Our biblical stories offer a spectrum of concepts of home. Eden was the perfect home from which Adam and Eve were banished for wanting more than everything they needed. Noah made home in a boat, a crowded place of redemption. The people of Israel longed for home through multiple episodes of exile, willing to follow Moses for a generation in the desert to get to

1. Joan M. Teno, et al., "Change in End-of-Life Care for Medicare Beneficiaries: Site of Death, Place of Care, and Health Care Transitions in 2000, 2005, and 2009," *JAMA* 309 no. 5, (2013): 470–477, doi:10.1001/jama.2012.207624.

a home they believed was chosen especially for them by God, a promised land that was already a home to others. In the earliest gospel story, Joseph and Mary made a home for their newborn Jesus in a stranger's stable and then fled to make a home of safety in Egypt, away from family, friends, and the familiar. In the last years of his life, Jesus moved in and out of Galilee, and spent his ministry being taken into the homes of others. In one of the parables told by Jesus, home is the open arms of a father running down the road to greet his prodigal son.

Home, in our story as people of God, is more than a place of refuge or identity; it is the place where we are most aware of God's presence and guidance, and most accepting of God's love and protection. At times in our journeys, the earthly structures and shelters in which we live, work, and worship, however humble or grand, can represent this place for a time. Sometimes we have only our own bodies to call home, wherever they carry us in health or in sickness. Within us we carry always the deep mystery of the Child called Emmanuel, "God with us," who knew only a manger in which to lay his head.

My first experience of managing death at home was in sharing the care for my father, Jack. Long before hospice was widely available, he had made a choice to treat his lung cancer as long as he felt well and able to care for himself, and he did. For the long summer of my internship in family medicine, he drove himself every weekday to radiation therapy, maintaining his weight and his good spirits. When he developed a sudden breathlessness due to radiation pneumonitis over that Labor Day weekend, he agreed to an emergency trip to the hospital in the middle of the night. As the very brand new doctor in the family, though five hundred miles away, I was assigned to make the calls to the emergency room doctor and the family physician, interpreting their assessments and their treatment recommendations to my five siblings. Jack had a different notion, and told my mother that very morning to "take him home to die." All of his children came home to Atlanta, from as far away as Alaska, and Boston, and Germany, and took turns sitting, waiting, bathing, helping him up and down to a bedside commode, fixing him bourbon and coke with which to chase his pain pills, and honoring his wish to be in his small, un-air-conditioned house in a hot humid Georgia September for the last three weeks of his life. We set him up in the guest bedroom where he mostly slept, and asked for very little. On his last day he ate some homemade custard a close friend had brought, walked to his favorite chair to watch his birds outside the picture window, walked back to the bed he had shared with my mother for fifty-one years, took off his oxygen, and died. It would be many years later, long after being trained as a physician to squeeze the last bit of life out of anyone who presented to me for care, to appreciate the gift my father had given me and my family—the experience of gathering to witness to and assist in a peaceful death at home.

It is not an uncommon experience for members of a hospice team, including nurses, nursing assistants, chaplains, social workers, bereavement counselors and doctors, to be told by a patient nearing the end of life that they are *ready to go home*. When this message is relayed to other members of the care team, it is commonly asked if the patient means *home* (from the hospital, nursing home, or family member's house to the place where they remember being well and independent) or *home-home* (to die). *Home-home*, heaven in the language of faith, represents rest, whether from a life well lived or from a long period of struggle and suffering. This place of rest is described in the twenty-first chapter of the Book of Revelation:

> And I heard a loud voice from the throne saying,
> "See, the home of God is among mortals.
> He will dwell with them;
> they will be his peoples,
> and God himself will be with them;
> he will wipe every tear from their eyes.
> Death will be no more;
> mourning and crying and pain will be no more,
> for the first things have passed away."[2]

It is a great and painful gift to be present with someone who is dying in the sacred space of home, accompanied by loving family and caregivers.

Dying at home is something old that has become something new. Before medicine had so much to offer to extend lives beyond the insults of heart disease, infections, cancers and "the thousand natural shocks that flesh is heir to,"[3] people died at home, cared for by their families. With the rise of the power of medicine in modern Western life came the rise of the power of the hospital as a place to access reversal of illness and, by association, of death. There was a time when doctor and priest were called to the home as someone was ill or seemed to be approaching death. After death, the body was laid out in the home prior to burial, and family and friends were received into the home to share the burden of grief. There were pain and grief and trauma for sure

---

2. Revelation 21:3–4 NRSV.

3. Shakespeare, *Hamlet*, Yale editions, eds. Tucker Brooke and Jack Randall Crawford (New Haven: Yale UP), 3.1. 62–63.

in the loss of someone loved; this depth of feeling cannot be romanticized away. However, the difference between then and now is that now, by the time a patient and family choose death at home, usually with home hospice services, they have already experienced weeks to months of hospitalizations, surgeries, therapies, and prolonged disruptions in work, strained relationships with family, and lost time with friends, recreation, and travel. This trajectory of serious illness has already involved a thousand negotiations and decisions involving multiple health-care teams and physicians. Often the experience is likened to a battle with the disease, with death as the ultimate enemy. Small victories have given rise to hope for many more in an extended campaign, buffered by enough advances in science to offer a more prolonged prognosis than possible in even the previous generation. By the time disease becomes very advanced and every possible treatment has been offered and tried, including some that had little evidence of holding off the dying process, and some that may actually have in their toxicity hastened it, patients and their caregivers are spent. There has been so little talk of the inevitable progression of the terminal disease that reaching the place of "nothing else we can do" is as shocking as reaching a dead end on a long road that was meant to be a short cut. In following the "miracles of modern medicine," we have lost our way home.

The National Hospice and Palliative Care Organization reports that the average length of stay in an American hospice program in 2014 for all diagnoses was around seventy-one days from admission to death. This included elderly patients with the slow wasting decline of dementia, strokes, heart failure, chronic lung disease, and cancers. The median length of service in hospice care was seventeen days, meaning that half of all patients in

2014 who chose it received hospice care for less than seventeen days, and half received care for more than seventeen days, often after months to years of aggressive disease-directed treatment.[4] Many people do not seek or consent to hospice care to assist with their dying until they are in the last two or three days of life. The significance of these numbers is that, even though many studies report that most Americans would prefer to die at home, peacefully surrounded by loved ones, with their affairs in order, very few of us approach this option with any clarity of planning or purpose.[5] Many people believe that "when you sign up for hospice, you will be dead in two days"; they are right, but only because it becomes a self-fulfilling prophecy. Fear of this outcome keeps people from accessing expert assistance in symptom management, caregiving strategies and help, and the psychosocial and spiritual support to which they are entitled in their dying until there is barely time for patients and their families to even understand what is happening—that the end of a life is very near. They wait until they are overwhelmed by their own exhaustion or shocked into needing immediate help with weakness, pain, or incontinence. When they finally agree to the offer of help from hospice, the decision is often preceded by profound anxiety, anger, and resentment towards their specialist health care providers, who either had never offered the approach of comfort care, or were not heard when they did. This anxiety, anger, and resentment is often transferred to hospice

4. National Palliative Care Organization, "NHPCO's Facts and Figures: Hospice Care in America" (2015), *http://www.nhpco.org/sites/default/files/public/Statistics_Research/2015_Facts_Figures.pdf*.

5. Amber E. Barnato, MD, et al., "Are Regional Variations in End-of-Life Care Intensity Explained by Patient Preferences? A Study of the US Medicare Population," *Med Care* 45, no. 5 (2007): 386–393, doi:10.1097/01.mlr.0000255248.79308.41.

workers when there is little time to establish relationships, offer support, and educate about a different and more comfortable way to live at the end of life. Hospice, the "H" word, becomes synonymous with "giving up," which can be viewed as the gravest sin of one experiencing life-threatening illness, or of caregivers when patients are too sick to speak for themselves. Even within our love-hate relationship with American health care, we as consumers believe that there will always be one more thing that can be done, one more treatment that has not been tried or offered, or in the case of insistence on prolonged life support, one more answer that has yet to be discovered—that will come along if we can only keep the body alive long enough.

We are all headed *home-home* eventually. Our mortality is as certain as our immortality. Within the context of Christian belief we move through our rituals of acting out this reality in Baptism (*There is one Body and one Spirit; There is one hope in God's call to us; One Lord, one Faith, one Baptism; One God and Father of all*),[6] in the Eucharist (*In the fullness of time, put all things in subjection under your Christ, and bring us to that heavenly country where, with all your saints, we may enter the everlasting heritage of your sons and daughters*),[7] in the liturgical rhythms of Lent and Easter, in the deposition of ashes on our foreheads at Ash Wednesday (*Remember that you are dust, and to dust you shall return*).[8] We profess in the Nicene Creed that *we look for the resurrection of the dead, and the life of the world to come.*[9] In the service of burial in the Book of Common Prayer, we say,

---

6. The Episcopal Church, *The Book of Common Prayer* (New York: Seabury Press, 1979), 299.

7. Ibid., 369.

8. Ibid., 265.

9. Ibid., 359.

For none of us has life in himself,
and none becomes his own master when he dies.
For if we have life, we are alive in the Lord,
and if we die, we die in the Lord.
So, then, whether we live or die,
we are the Lord's possession.[10]

And yet what we know to be true in the collective becomes only relatively true in the particular—for surely God cannot be ready for *us* to come home *now*?

Over years of sitting with people at their dying time, I have heard many patients and families speak a common language of heaven as a literal place where they will see God face to face, and see loved ones who have died before them. I have witnessed not infrequently a dying patient describe someone in the room, that no one else can see, present and waiting to go with them to where they are going when they let go. It might be mother, or grandmother, or angels, or Jesus. This experience affirms a sense of returning to someplace familiar, rather than of going away to someplace strange, and it gives both the dying and their loved ones comfort and peace.

How do our memories of home color our sense of what happens when we die? Do we truly believe that our Father's house has many dwelling places, and that Jesus has gone to prepare a place for us? Is heaven a physical place, where we will hear God's voice calling us as if home for supper? And if that eternal home we sing about is as wonderful as we have been taught to believe, a home where we will know perfect peace, what does our God make of our clinging to this life, of our fear of letting go? How can we live in anticipation—in joyful hope—of our eventual return to the Source of our being, as the river meets the sea?

---

10. Ibid., 491.

CHAPTER 3

Why Me?

> So teach us to number our days
>> that we may apply our hearts to wisdom.
>
> —PSALM 90:12 BCP

I met Gloria in her ninety-fifth year, when she was admitted to the inpatient hospice unit where I was working after her symptoms of congestive heart failure did not improve with prolonged and repeated hospitalizations (of which she had little memory), including many weeks in intensive care units. She was alert and oriented to everything, gregarious and funny, and had, until her most recent hospitalization, lived independently (more or less) in between her medical crises. She had admittedly had a wonderful and enviable life, having been married and widowed twice, both times to wealthy men with whom she had traveled the world. She spoke often of her adventures and of the notebooks she had filled over the years describing her adventures. She had children and grandchildren who adored her and were attentive and frequently present and expected her to live forever. By the time I met Gloria, she needed continuous oxygen, yet was short of breath with moving, speaking, and eating. Her heart was performing at only a small fraction of its peak performance, and no amount of fine-tuning her optimal medications could coax any more out of it. She could not tolerate being out of bed due to her severe weakness, so decided to live well in it. Her bed was covered in homemade quilts. She was always dressed in elegant dressing gowns and insisted on her make-up and hair being just right every day. Her tray table was always laden with elegant candies for her guests. She quickly became a favorite of the staff. But after a few days, Gloria became impatient with all the attention. What she truly wanted was her life and her independence back. She wanted to turn back the clock. And she wanted to live to be a hundred. She said she believed in God and believed she had been a good person in this life, and therefore her burning question to me about her illness and seemingly short prognosis was, *Why me?*

I had heard this question before and have heard it many times since. It is a universal hypothetical wail of human frustration, dissatisfaction, or suffering. The question implies its corollaries: *Why this?* and *Why now?*, inferring that whatever ill wind or evil has befallen us has somehow landed upon us unfairly and intentionally, possibly by God's design. The question also implies an understanding that bad things happen to some people some of the time, including the bad thing of dying, but that *some* people should not include *me* or the people I love, *at least not yet*. That the question *Why me?* had been asked by someone of generous years, who had lived by all accounts a charmed life, merely holds it up with enough irony to give it poignancy. Not everyone who is challenged by illness or trauma asks this question out loud in exactly those two words; some ask it quietly through their tears; some hide it in their anger, shock, or disappointment. Some ask it only with their eyes. It is a question that crosses boundaries of age, race, class, and culture. This question may have been asked through all human time, yet I hear it in a contemporary American context.

To answer this question, to address the failure of the body in ways that can be understood by anyone who is not a medical professional, requires metaphoric language. I explained to Gloria that her heart functioned like a pump and her pump was worn out from over ninety-five years of faithful service, and that this part could not be replaced because her other highly-worn parts (lungs, kidneys, and blood vessels) could not survive the strain of a new replacement heart (yes, she asked about this possibility). I did not assault her with the ethical argument that the expense and sacrifice involved in transplantation of organs could only be justified in patients with some reasonable life expectancy in the first place. I carefully explained that every possible medication and treatment known and available had been given to her already, and that some of these had already extended her life beyond its natural course. She accepted this medical reasoning with calm disappointment, and I saw her release the hope that lived in her imagination that surely in America, with what she believed to be the best medical system in the world, there was something else, something that up until now had been withheld from her, that would be the cure for her, once again holding off her death until some indefinite time in the future.

I have witnessed thousands of people with serious illness who, along with their family members, hold on to this hope. It is fueled by stories of miracles, of personal experiences of unexpected reprieve from what seemed a certain end, and by the human capacity to value the existence of a future in this world far beyond any accommodation of suffering required to sustain it. I believe this hope may have been born in our species in a genetic animal drive to survive, though it persists in a collective expectation that arises from a privileged society that worships its science and technology. Some of us live to a very old age, having escaped the random insults of infectious disease, trauma, and a genetic predisposition to chronic debilitating illnesses. Some of us have access to available and affordable medications and treatments that prolong survival from those chronic illnesses, including everything from life coaching and nutritional counseling to kidney dialysis, joint and organ replacements, and artificial nutrition and respiratory support. All of these things support our hope for a longer and/or better life. For Gloria, this list of possibilities had been exhausted, and she was exhausted. She was no less devastated in facing the end of her life than the forty-one-year-old down the hall, and she folded into herself for a day or so, taking in this reality, that the end of her life was near.

The harder question to address for Gloria was why God would want her to die. Gloria professed a Christian faith and believed that she would go to heaven when she died. She did not have a clear vision of what heaven looked like or what she would do there, but she believed that it would be a reward for living a good life; she was just not ready for that good life to be over. Offering her new and challenging theological discussions about what the Book of Wisdom calls the secret purposes of God (Wisd. of Sol. 2:22) would not have been helpful in her stage of physical weakness, for how could she accept that God willed her to suffer?

What did help Gloria to face her death without fear were the Psalms, read to her by the chaplain and hospice volunteers. She loved the twenty-third Psalm, but it was Psalm 24 that took her to a very peaceful place:

> The earth is the LORD's and all that is in it,
>   the world and all who dwell therein.

For it is he who founded it upon the seas
    and made it firm upon the rivers of the deep.
"Who can ascend the hill of the LORD?
    and who can stand in his holy place?"
"Those who have clean hands and a pure heart,
    who have not pledged themselves to falsehood,
    nor sworn by what is a fraud.
They shall receive a blessing from the LORD
    and a just reward for the God of their salvation."

                 —PSALM 24:1–5 BCP

Words of medical explanation helped Gloria to understand that there was a physiologic reason that she would likely not live much longer, and that there was no human remedy that would mend her heart and keep it beating. It was the words of the Psalms that gave her life context, that helped her to see herself as part of a larger whole of all of God's creation, and that, ill or well, she was in God's care, as were the rivers and the seas, indeed the whole world that she had been blessed to see with her own eyes. It gave her rest that the God of her salvation honored her pure heart and that she had already received God's blessing.

    Within a few days of her arrival at the hospice inpatient center, Gloria's heart grew so weak that she barely had the energy to speak. She had called for her daughter to come, and gave her specific instructions for finding her last travelogue book, which had been treasured in a very specific cabinet in her home. Gloria wanted it brought to her, along with her suitcase, because she was about to take one last trip. Her last few days of life were spent sleeping peacefully with her shortness of breath well controlled with comfort medications, and with her travelogue lying next to her in the bed. All of her trips had been recorded there except for the one she was about to take. This last journey had never been on her wish list, yet she had made up her mind to get herself packed and prepared, say her goodbyes, and wait peacefully for her departure.

It has been my experience that very few people approach death without fear and anxiety, regardless of having had a long life well-lived. In one of my earliest experiences in palliative care, I found myself with my team's social worker and chaplain, sitting across a table with two daughters of a hundred-year-old woman who was languishing in an intensive care unit. Her children were in their seventies, but nowhere near ready to choose a comfort plan of care for their mother. "I know my mother is not ready to go yet," one of the daughters kept repeating, making it clear that it was *she* who was not ready to let go of the medical-technological interventions that were keeping her mother alive but unable to make her well. If one hundred years are not enough, how many years would be?

Americans and others who can access the lifetime benefits of Western medicine are living longer and older. We are surviving many chronic illnesses that meant certain death in just the last century. We are replacing our parts and sharing our organs with others, and science is even now working on ways to re-grow parts of ourselves that have worn out, and on techniques to correct our genetic mutations of accident or insult that program our illnesses. We have not had many conversations in the context of community on what this means—not only to any one of us but to all of us. Does God expect or delight in us striving to outwit our finitude? Do we believe that immortality is a virtue, and how does that shape the way we live our lives? If we believe we will have infinite time in the future to mend our fences, change our ways, to repent and to forgive, what will prompt us to love, to reconciliation, to redemption where we are now? Do we appreciate summer without winter, or Easter without Good Friday, or life without death?

CHAPTER 4

Are You Just Going to Let Me Die?

Martha said to Jesus, "Lord, if you had been here, my brother would not have died."

—John 11:21

Miko was angry. She was forty-eight, yellow, thin and weak, but mostly she was angry. She was angry at her husband, at her son, at every doctor that had ever tried to help her, at her hospice nurse, and at me. She had pancreatic cancer that had been treated with major surgery, radiation, and multiple rounds of chemotherapy, and she had lived for three years since being first diagnosed. Her last year of life could be attributed to two permanent drains that drained the bile from her minimally functioning liver. Each one came out of the right side of her belly and drained into its own bag and both had been changed out more than fifteen times, a procedure performed by a medical specialist called an interventional radiologist. This specialty did not exist when I was a younger physician; most of the things they do, which not so long ago were saved for the skill of the surgeon, are made possible by advances in the technology of imaging—scans of all types that create windows into the body. The tools of the interventional radiologist are used to diagnose and to treat illness, both by extracting what is causing trouble and by inserting

33

what might aid in healing—all while being able to see what they are doing without opening up the patient wider than the hole made by a needle.

Miko had experienced the best of what interventional radiology had to offer, and had far exceeded her prognosis. Whenever her hospice team (including myself) tried to discuss her decline with her, we were met with "I need to live one or two more years," even though her life was defined by confinement to her couch, and pain and nausea for which she refused medication. When she began to have leaking around the insertion site of her tubes, and when multiple trips to the radiology suite could not resolve the problem because of enlarging metastatic tumors encompassing her liver, Miko began to die. And she was very angry. She refused to accept that the risks of repeated tube insertions were greater than any benefit she might receive. She was convinced that everyone was conspiring to withhold some treatment from her that would prolong her life those "one or two years." Miko's husband had to work in order to maintain her health insurance, and could do nothing to help her in her misery. He was frustrated by her wailing demands to be taken to the hospital interspersed with her demands to remain at home. Their son lived far away, with small children and a business to run, and could not be present for long periods. Miko fired personal caregivers and berated the hospice nursing assistants who came to bathe her. And she screamed at her nurse, accusing her of "letting her die."

Miko professed a Christian faith, but refused to see the chaplain. She took communion brought to her by the local Catholic church but would not talk to the priest. She walled herself off in her misery and threw disappointment and grief on anyone who approached her ramparts. Why was she so angry? Had life failed her so miserably, and if so, why would she want more of it?

Good training and a compassionate heart are the basic tools with which a nurse, social worker, chaplain, or physician walks into the lives of patients like Miko. The hospice team knows by experience the suffering that comes with pain, nausea, constipation, seizures, hiccups, and other physical discomforts and have sure remedies to bring relief if patient and caregiver are willing to try what is offered. Emotional symptoms of depression, anxiety, grief, family dysfunction, mental illness, and substance abuse are more challenging, yet can improve with attention and trust built into an ongoing relationship among patient, family, caregiver, and a hospice team. Existential spiritual distress in a patient is the most difficult to address, even for the chaplain trained in end-of-life work, as it expresses a deep, and sometimes lifelong, loss of meaning and purpose brought to the surface when life is threatened by illness, debility, and impending death.

Loss of control over one's own body creates a free fall into loss of the soul. Weakness, fatigue, pain; the disfiguration from surgeries; attachment of tubes, drains, or bags; giving up driving and mobility are all losses that can lead to an abyss of powerlessness. Losses in self-care—from cooking to bathing, dressing and toileting; loss of purposeful work or meaningful play; loss of a clear head and the trust of loved ones to make good decisions—all are wounds that undermine self-confidence, self-determination, self-dignity. Without some deep spiritual grounding, these losses, compounded by emotional distress or strained relationships, can create deep existential suffering.

In Miko's mind, the remedy for her suffering would be the restoration of her life, ideally a rewind to the time before she was ill. Ironically, though she admitted to experiencing pain, she often refused to use the pain medications available to her. She wanted to live, even in her state of decline. She was unable to speak to her desire with any more detail or depth, and she became angry with anyone who tried to prepare her for her impending death. She wanted repetition of treatments that had been determined to be medically ineffective, and when she was denied these futile treatments she took up her mantra, "Are you just going to let me die?"

I have come to believe that there is a bit of Miko in each one of us, and it comes out in varying degrees when we are faced with mortality—our own or that of someone we are trying desperately to care for. We want the bad thing *not* to be happening, and because it is unfolding painfully slowly (as opposed to quickly and traumatically) we believe that the bad thing can be controlled, *if only*. . . . *If only* we were offered another treatment like the one that worked in the past; *if only* we had tried a different medical center; *if only* our insurance had covered that experimental procedure; *if only* I had tried those herbal remedies our neighbor offered; *if only* I had prayed harder; *if only* I had been a better person. Regret feeds the pain and does not heal it. Regret feeds the anger and turns itself upon the one who suffers and those who suffer with her.

When faced with the challenge of caring for Miko, patience and compassion and loving-kindness seemed inadequate tools. It is hard to walk into someone else's pain with every good intention of becoming a healing presence and instead becoming the primary repository of frustration, disappointment, and despair. It is hard to be handed the responsibility of "just letting someone die." In Miko's case, her hospice team stuck it out with her and her bewildered husband, along with the caregivers the family hired very late in Miko's illness. Liver failure eventually made Miko more confused and then sleepy, and she finally accepted some small amount of pain medication, which allowed her to be more comfortable. She just wore herself down and wore out. Her son was able to come for her last few days of life, to support his mother in her dying and his father in his grieving. Miko's death was peaceful at the very last, but only because her body finally failed her and her energy to resist her death was gone. In the end, we did all "just let her die."

It is tempting to believe that we were not helpful to Miko because we were not able to give her "one or two more years," and because our care for her could not be compromised by lying to her, no matter how much she wanted just that. The call to be a faithful presence in the face of anger and disappointment is not one often sought. The experience brings to mind the story in the Book of Job of his friends of who sit with him, initially, in silent witness to his suffering:

> Now when Job's three friends heard of all these troubles that had come upon him, each of them set out from his home— Eliphaz the Temanite, Bildad the Shuhite, and Zophar the Naamathite. They met together to go and console and comfort him. When they saw him from a distance, they did not recognize him, and they raised their voices and wept aloud; they tore their robes and threw dust in the air upon their heads. They sat with him on the ground for seven days and seven nights, and no one spoke a word to him, for they saw that his suffering was very great.
>
> —Job 2:11–13

Eventually Job's friends can't handle his suffering any more, and begin to argue with him that he must have sinned, done something unrighteous, to bring such pain upon himself. It is too difficult for them to believe that his losses and illnesses could have been visited upon Job in any random fashion not of his own deserving; if that were true they would be just as vulnerable to the same calamities. Because Job persists in declaring his innocence, they distance themselves from him, finding it frighteningly impossible to remain as silent witnesses to Job's undoing.

It is this same human longing for reason and explanation, physical or spiritual, that can undermine our caring and support of others. We sense that despair is contagious, and we keep our distance: physically, emotionally and spiritually. We believe that our own sense of helplessness in the face of another's suffering is detrimental, and so we shield ourselves from the pain we see in others as they are dying. I believe it is this self-preserving invisible wall of distance from others that leads the dying person to feel abandoned; the experience of "letting die" is an expression of the awareness of this abandonment. Job felt this abandonment when he was blamed for his own suffering, and it cut him off completely until he prayed to die. At the end of Job's story, God steps in and sets things right—admonishing Job's friends and restoring Job to health, but only after Job prays for his friends who were mistaken in their assessment of his afflictions. Had Job's friends been able to continue to sit and suffer with him as they did in the beginning, perhaps Job's suffering would have been diminished by their sharing, rather than compounded by their blaming of Job that was born of their own fear and anxiety.

The lesson from Job's story, and from Miko's story, at first seems counter-intuitive. To just sit and listen—to be silently

present for the wailing and the complaints and the despair—
would seem to be less than what might be called for. To just
sit and "do nothing" feels like "just letting them die." When
someone has already received all known and conceivable treatment intended to reverse illness, when the only medicine left
is intended to maintain physical comfort, it is very hard to just
be with someone in that place of dawning recognition that her
life span is short. To just listen to someone mourn his own life
without commentary or conjecture is challenging. To just sit
with someone loved and needed in our own lives, while quieting
our own fear of loss, is near to impossible without the strong
conviction that God has all things under God's care, even when
the suffering one is crying out in anger or despair.

Where do we find the courage to stop beating on the door of
the hospital looking for something that does not exist to cure an
incurable illness? Where do we find the grace to accept that all
that could be done has been done, and that for the dying to die
peacefully, we need to move—slowly, deliberately, faithfully—to
a place where the need to fix can be let go, and where the blessing found in sitting and waiting can be embraced? How can we
re-learn that our hubris in health care does not give us power over
life and death? Who can convince us that leaving a stone unturned
in the treatment of a dying loved one is not akin to murder? How
do we beat the swords of our fight against death into plowshares,
cultivating a sacred space for dying that honors all that a life has
meant? Where do we turn for the healing presence of God, at
whose feet all the anger and frustration and despair can be laid?
Where do we find the space that invites repentance and forgiveness and reconciliation to old wounds of relationship—the space
that invites suffering to leave, and the sufferer to die in peace?

CHAPTER 5

Ruler of the Heart

For God alone my soul in silence waits;
   from him comes my salvation.
He alone is my rock and my salvation,
   my stronghold, so that I shall not be greatly shaken.
                              —Psalm 62:1–2 BCP

Jordan entered the inpatient hospice center where I was working after he experienced an episode of bleeding at home from a late-stage cancerous tumor in his neck that had progressed in spite of an aggressive treatment plan of surgery, radiation, and chemotherapies. He had been given a tracheostomy, a permanent hole in the front of his throat in order to breathe, as the tumor had invaded his upper airway. Because of the tracheostomy and the tumor, he was unable to swallow, and had a feeding tube placed directly into his stomach through the skin, fat, and muscles of his abdomen in order to receive nourishment. Other than these insults to his forty-year-old body, he was handsome, engaging, and charming. He smiled freely and did not complain, communicating his needs with pen and paper. His demeanor was almost regal, and it was clear he was in charge of what went on in his room. He was able to walk around but spent most of his time in his automatic bed with the back raised, giving the impression he was sitting comfortably on a throne. Even though he was seated, it was clear he was tall; he held himself upright with his chin raised, perhaps partly due to the tracheostomy. He performed all of his own trach care, changing the inner cannula, cleaning it, and self-suctioning. He did his own feedings through the tube inserted into his stomach, and was on more than one occasion found using alcoholic drinks, or grinding up pound cake and milk to force into the tube, because he could "taste" it when he belched. He clearly missed eating. He did not seem to be ill enough to be in an inpatient unit, but he was at high risk for a recurrence of bleeding from a major blood vessel in his neck close to his progressive tumor; if the bleeding were massive it would immediately compromise his airway and end his life.

Jordan was affable, alert, mischievous, oriented, and in charge of his destiny, calling on the hospice nurses only for treatment of his pain. But he was not alone. His room was always—24/7—filled with women. Young, middle-aged, and old, mostly tall and beautiful, and comprising a sisterhood of his current significant other, an ex-wife, an aunt, a mother, daughters and step-daughters, nieces, and friends. Each of them was devoted to their patient, fetching and attending, running errands, and generally sitting at his feet. They all got along with each other, quietly present to fill Jordan's every need. He was remarkably kind and affectionate to each of them, and they lived in a kind of private kingdom inside his room, where they loved and cared for this regal, beautiful man. They were the transporters of his alcohol, and they were the grinders of his homemade pound cake and milk, making sure his PEG tube did not clog with the mixture. They bathed him, changed his linens, played his favorite music, read to him, and made him feel adored. Jordan was so well attended that it felt almost intrusive to visit him on rounds. Nevertheless, nurses and volunteers, chaplains and social workers all fell in love with him, in that way that hospice workers allow only a very few patients to break their hearts. Everyone on a hospice team seems to know who these patients are on first meeting; when told by a team member that a new patient "will break your heart," it is code for those special people who touch professional caregivers more deeply than most; the ones who come with the uncanny ability to tap into longstanding collective barrels of grief.

The dignity that Jordan displayed in the hospice unit was not assigned to him by the people who worked there, though their training had given them tools to affirm the dignity of every dying patient they encountered. This particular patient brought it with him, and it commanded a quiet appreciation of who he was beneath the disease that had ravaged his beautiful body and was cutting short his life. This dignity was evident even at the moment of his death when the tumor finally and without warning eroded into a major artery in his neck, and Jordan began to bleed profusely. He did not reach for one of the dark burgundy towels on hand just in case; he did not cry out in panic. He did get out of bed and walk into the bathroom, where he sat down on the floor of the shower stall. The women who loved him crowded into the bathroom and held his hands as he bled out and died within a few minutes. He did not want to cause a mess that would have been difficult to clean up or to forget. He died with more dignity on the floor of that shower than I had ever seen before, or have seen since.

It is fully appropriate to access available and non-life-threatening treatments that extend a life with acceptable quality, to beat back an insult to the body that restores a person to wholeness and strength, even for a limited time. Jordan's tracheostomy and feeding tube gave him a little more "quality time" with an attentive and adoring family, and Jordan was in control of that life. Admittedly, it is a dangerous business to judge quality of life in another; I have found that there is a fathomless capacity in humans to accept decline in stages and learn to live with much less function over time. One person's acceptable existence is another person's hell on earth, and we have poor language to have conversation about these issues.

And yet I have also seen an unfathomable capacity of some to become immune to the suffering of others, especially those they profess to love and care for, availing themselves of any and all life-prolonging measures to sustain a life that has been reduced to misery and pain that is neither acknowledged nor addressed. I am forever haunted by the anxiety and pain in the eyes of Susie, an elderly woman with a severe end-stage neurodegenerative disease whose spouse was reluctant to treat her non-verbal but severe signs of distress. She would make a high pitched keening noise when moved or touched, which was required frequently to clean and dress her many pressure wounds. She had to be suctioned frequently from her long-term tracheostomy, which made her eyes go wide with fear.

"She's fine, she always makes that noise; it stops when you leave her alone," or "She's not in pain, and anyway, I don't like to give her medicine because it makes her sleep," were his responses, and *he* was in charge. She received just enough artificial nutrition through her feeding tube to sustain a cachectic, contracted, and completely dependent existence, because any more than that caused aspiration pneumonia or diarrhea. If the hospice team challenged Susie's husband about his care decisions too strongly, he pushed back, and there was a fear he would kick the care team out, leaving her in even more dire circumstances. When she ran a fever or her urine was cloudy in her Foley catheter bag, he would call an ambulance and have her transported to the emergency room, revoking her hospice benefit and looking for something the hospice team had not been providing—something heroic to extend her life: diagnostic tests, IV antibiotics, or mechanical ventilation in the ICU. Do caregivers like Susie's husband acclimate to a terrible situation so slowly that they no longer experience the distress seen by an outside observer? Is it fear of death, or fear of the loss of another to death, that blinds us, and binds us, to the suffering of another? Is it a failure of the imagination to reinvent a life without the identity of caregiver, with all of its assignments of heroism or martyrdom, that finds us clinging to another's life? Is it the terror of being alone, when the tapestry of our former friendships in the world has worn thin in the isolation and attention-consuming period of our caregiving? Is it the guilt born of a long wounded relationship that sends us seeking redemption as defender of the dying, championing futile treatments for those with little life left, where benefit is small and burden is great? Is it the fear of a loved one dying without our having done enough? When we pray for the suffering one to keep living, whatever the cost, who is the prayer for?

Application of futile treatments becomes the communally demoralizing lie that erodes the joy in the work of health care while causing pain to those with little life left; risk is high, benefit is small, and the financial burden is great. Many hospitalizations and invasive treatments offered to the increasingly ill, and especially to the frail elderly, hold minimal benefit in restoration of function or comfort, and yet they are expected, insisted upon, given, and paid for—dearly paid for—by families and by all of us. The Kaiser

Family Foundation reports that roughly one-quarter of traditional Medicare spending for health care is for services provided to Medicare beneficiaries in their last year of life—a proportion that has remained steady for decades.[1] The CBS news show *60 Minutes* reported in 2009 that the cost of care in the last two months of life for Medicare beneficiaries was $50 billion, more than the combined budgets of Homeland Security and the Department of Education for that year.[2] Hospice utilization has increased for elderly Medicare recipients from 26 to 47 percent between 2002 and 2012, yet some of these hospice admissions occur only after prolonged intensive care hospitalizations.[3] A critical conversation awaits us about both the quality of these decisions and the stewardship of our collective resources they represent.

Our medical culture, supported by our American cultural sense of privilege (whether we are medically insured or not) has nurtured in us a sense of power over death with a concomitant right of access to any and all resources to support that power. Dignity in the face of illness and disease has been confused and co-opted by the metaphor of fighting an enemy who is death, as if dignity is defined by the fighting spirit of a warrior and by the "best available" resources that warrior expends in the battle. Love becomes confused with a willingness to put the beloved through

---

1. Tricia Neuman, et al., "The Rising Cost of Living Longer: Analysis of Medicare Spending by Age for Beneficiaries in Traditional Medicare," Kaiser Family Foundation, January 14, 2015, *http://kff.org/medicare/report/the-rising-cost-of-living-longer-analysis -of-medicare-spending-by-age-for-beneficiaries-in-traditional-medicare/*.

2. "The Cost of Dying," *CBS News*, November 19, 2009, *http://www.cbsnews.com /news/the-cost-of-dying/*.

3. Christopher Hogan, Direct Research LLC for the Medicare Payment Advisory Commission, "Spending in the Last Year of Life and the Impact of Hospice on Medicare Outlays," (2015) *http://medpac.gov/documents/contractor-reports/spending-in-the -last-year-of-life-and-the-impact-of-hospice-on-medicare-outlays-rev.pdf*.

any and all available medical treatments, including second and third opinions, and resistance to recommendations for treatment based on prognosis and focused on comfort. Maximum accessible treatments are demanded, regardless of the suffering they cause, to prove that love. Surrender is likened to cowardice; acceptance is anathema. True dignity is lost on the battlefield.

Is there dignity in forcing a ninety-seven-year-old man to be transported by stretcher to undergo dialysis three times a week when the rest of his time is spent sleeping and fighting with caregivers to be left alone? Is there dignity in the artificial feeding of an elderly woman for months or years—a woman who never leaves the dark room of a nursing home, having been devastated by a stroke without ability to move, or to speak, or to swallow, or to smile, or to recognize others? Is there dignity in robbing her of her ability to die in peace? Is there dignity in sustaining a body beyond its ability to maintain even the integrity of its own skin, breaking down into multiple sores just from the bed it lies in? Is clinging to a life beyond all measure of comfort or meaning considered courageous and dignified?

In earlier times in human history (prior to the wide availability of medical interventions covered by insurance or other providers), family and friends prepared for a loved one to die; part of that death was the stopping of eating and drinking. Is the shift to dependence on life-sustaining technology to feed always within the will of God? With what language should we discuss these questions and seek their answers?

Jordan and many other patients have taught me that surrender can be a powerful, loving act. We were created to live a life in a body that we will not know forever. Each and every one of us will die. If we believe in a life everlasting, we trust that our

God will be with us and our loved ones in the dying and in what comes after, just as our God is in each living breath we take. How can we find our way to the blessed assurance of knowing when we need to let go of suffering and await death in peace? How can we begin to speak of illness, and of dying and of death, with a different kind of courage that lays aside the fear of not having done enough for our dying ones? How can we support each other in these times of trial, reminding each other that God is with us, and does not demand suffering beyond reason to prove that we have loved life? How do we pray for healing of our fear of death?

CHAPTER 6

Please Leave Me Alone

He rained down manna upon them to eat
and gave them grain from heaven.

So mortals ate the bread of angels;
he provided for them food enough.

—Psalm 78:24–25 BCP

Willow was a dancer. Her given name was Rachel but at some time early in her career in ballet she thought it weighed her down and she began to call herself Willow, which was much more descriptive. She began to dance as a tiny girl and started ballet classes at age four, like many of her friends. For Willow, however, dance was not just something to occupy her energy and give her mother a break. Dancing became her life early on, and she danced at every opportunity. She did not complain about the punishing exercises and took her recitals seriously. She begged for more classes until she was living in a world of dance as an adolescent. School was a trial for her, wasted hours until she could be in the studio. She walked like a dancer, breathed like a dancer, and looked like a dancer with limbs as thin and limber as a willow tree.

By the age of fourteen Willow was very thin, much to the consternation of her mother, who, from the eyes of her Jewish heritage, saw herself as a failure for not being able to adequately feed her child. Willow became pale with dark circles under her eyes, and thin. And thinner.

For some years, she managed to keep dancing. Willow was rewarded for her passion and her skill, her lithe body and bruised toes, with praise and successful auditions for dancing roles, and as the rhythm of her life was set to the seasonal ballet productions in her city, she learned to keep her hunger caged in self-discipline. And she grew tall and angular and thinner.

Rachel's mother, for she refused to call her Willow, was proud of her daughter with the black glossy hair and translucent skin, whose name was in so many programs. On stage she was light and free as a bird, something ethereal; at home she wore baggy sweaters over her tights, and spent most of her time in her room, catching up on homework and sleep. Rachel's mother unsuccessfully badgered her to sit down to the table with her parents and brother to eat. When she caught a glimpse of her daughter unclothed through a cracked open door, she was shocked enough to think of the stories handed down by her family members of starvation in the camps in Germany during the war. When she confronted Rachel she was met with a teenager's defiance, and told to leave her alone. Willow connected her need to dance with her need to be thin. Neither she nor her mother considered that had they sought care early on, Willow would have been diagnosed with anorexia.

When Willow began to falter and faint in her late teens, she could no longer keep up with the physically rigorous workouts and rehearsals required to advance into a career of dance. Her father died unexpectedly and her mother was too absorbed in her grief to notice that Rachel was drifting away. The first time she was found unresponsive on the floor of her bedroom, Willow was hospitalized and initially force-fed, then transferred to inpatient psychiatric care where therapy was begun for anorexia. This was the beginning of a pattern that repeated for the next fifteen years of her life. Having lost the world of dance, and without any other world to replace it, Willow was mostly depressed. She had never cultivated long or sustaining relationships. She was unable to grieve the death of her father, with whom she had a complex and unhealthy history. She had no ambition or desire in the world. Willow's issues demanded so much of her mother's energy that Willow's only sibling, a brother, became estranged from the family, and made a life of his own, outside of a world of trying to keep Willow alive against her will. They had never been close.

By her early thirties, Willow had been hospitalized more than twenty times and been to many therapists. She had periods of relative stability, and was able to take some college classes, hold down a non-challenging job, or live with a roommate, but always after several months or a year she would slide back into the darkness and isolation of anorexia. She would function as best she could and then crash, each crash involving her mother's intervention: having her hospitalized, fed against her will when she was too ill to protest, and pushed back into intensive therapy. She had feeding tubes placed in her stomach against her will on more than one occasion; even this did not restore her to health.

After each of these traumatic episodes she was weaker and older and more tired, and she wanted it all to stop. She did not want to die, not at first; eventually she became too weary of feeling tired and ill, and exhausted from the battles. She began to sustain irreversible damage to her body: her mind became dull, her behavior became ever more childlike. And she could not eat.

What was considered initially psychiatric became physiologic, and finally Willow could not hold down, digest, or process food even if she had wanted to. She developed bleeding ulcers in her stomach resistant to treatment; she vomited frequently; she would go weeks without moving her bowels.

Willow moved into the inpatient hospice unit for care in the terminal phase of her recalcitrant illness, after many failed attempts at hospitalization with aggressive measures to reverse her malnutrition. She was tired and spent most of her time sleeping. She knew she was going to die, and did not wish her death to happen in the ICU on mechanical ventilation with tubes stuck down her nose and throat. Her mother was distraught; her brother was angry. Willow was very weak but wanted to walk, though she needed a child-size walker and the assistance of another person to hold her up. She kept her room very dark, lights off, curtains drawn. She had pain with any movement, and her skin broke down with minimal pressure. She weighed fifty-four pounds.

Occasionally, if the sun was warm, and if she was bundled up in layers of blankets over a wheelchair, Willow would allow someone to take her outside for a short while. Everyone in the hospice unit tried to reach her—the chaplain, the social worker, the nurses, the nursing assistants, the volunteers, and me, the doctor. It was hard to believe that enough love and attention to one so in need of it was not able to save Willow, who was disappearing before our eyes. All she would accept and partially consume was Diet Sprite, sugar-free Jell-O, and soft, kind, and soothing words. Her mother continued to bring in full meals, as if ever hoping to tempt her daughter out of some poorly understood spell. Inpatient staff struggled with her presence and her dying, seeing it as unethical, immoral, negligent, suicidal. That Willow was stubborn, withdrawn, and emotionally unreachable did not help. It was painful to see her, to watch her skeletal pacing in the halls hunched over her walker, to think about her young life wasted and wasting away.

One day, when Willow seemed to be responding to the warmth of the sun on the patio, I sat next to her, in what felt like an unholy silence. I was finally and completely at a loss for the words I prayed would save Willow, and I had stopped expecting to fix her. After a long period of quiet, she whispered, "I feel so heavy." It was such a shocking thing to hear from one who could have been made from the puff of a spent dandelion. Certainly a literal misconception, but it spoke of a heavy and difficult life burdened with failure, disappointment, and loss, as if she had been some other kind of spirit trapped in the wrong body for too long. She died in her sleep that night, quietly and peacefully.

Willow broke my heart, and the hearts of many others who cared for her. Her death tapped deeply into the community's collective well of grief because she was so young, and because her death was associated strongly in their minds with her refusal to eat, and the helplessness of many who tried to feed her.

One of the most difficult struggles I have witnessed in my time of caring for the dying is that of a caregiver who desires with a whole heart to nourish the one who is dying *with food*. This was true for Willow's mother; it is also true for caregivers of patients who have had a long struggle with cancer and its many debilitating treatments, or a sudden prognosis of advanced disease that had been masked by the patient's tolerance of its subtle incursion. It is true for those who witness the progressive decline of patients with degenerative neurological disease, who are losing their ability to swallow, or for those who have exhausted all available aggressive medical resources to treat failing hearts and lungs, using up their reserves of energy just to breathe, with none left over for chewing, swallowing, and digesting. And it is painfully true for those who care for one who has suffered the long, slow, heartbreaking journey of dementia in all of its many forms.

The need to feed one who does not desire to eat can become a source of tremendous stress between patients and their personal caregivers. Patients weakening from terminal disease will tell their spouse, their children, their caregivers and their hospice team repeatedly that they are *not* hungry, which can be received as rejection of a caregiver's best efforts. Some patients will eat to please others, even when it causes them physical distress. Other patients long for an appetite, and even request certain foods, sending family members on quests of shopping and cooking, and then pushing the plate away after one or two bites. Some patients with declining cognition will take in spoon-fed mouthfuls then hold the food in their cheek pockets because they have forgotten how to swallow; they cough and choke and suffer from recurrent aspiration, which leads to pneumonia and breathlessness. Rarely, particularly in the setting of advanced dementia, a patient will continue to eat just enough pureed spoonfuls of "baby food" to go on living—bed-bound, incontinent, with loss of speech and expression, loss of weight and muscle mass, loss of eye contact, loss of purposeful movement, and with development of tight fixed painful contractures of arms and legs. I once assumed care for a patient in this state of many losses who was painstakingly spoon fed even when it took hours to get in a cupful, and whose inevitable choking was countered with mechanical suction always at the ready. Food was placed in her mouth, and if she did not swallow and began to choke, the caregiver would suction it back out, and then commence to place the next spoon of food in her mouth. I did not see this patient show any signs of engagement with life in her last year of slowly wasting away, but the caregiver could not stop trying to feed her.

The relationship between caregiver and cared-for may be loving, difficult, intimate, estranged, or contractual, but the compulsion to feed is almost universal. The need and desire to feed supersedes all other caregiving demands, including cleaning and bathing, treating pain and other discomforts, and providing a clean and safe environment for one who is dying. The arguments I have heard supporting the effort to feed a dying person range from belief that it is the lack of food and drink causing the dying, to the belief that *not* eating and drinking is a primary source of physical suffering. When a personal caregiver assumes the responsibility for keeping a patient alive, the most visible and accessible way of living into that responsibility is to feed. Feeding is an expression of loving, and therefore it is assumed that *not* feeding becomes an indictment of *not* loving. This idea is reinforced by some religious leaders who have taught their people that not feeding, under any circumstances, is tantamount to killing. This belief can layer guilt and anguish over the already grief-stricken who are struggling with impending loss.

In a culture of high expectations of medical technology, when someone we love is failing, we look for solutions from technology, which tries not to disappoint. When we assume that everything that breaks in the body can be fixed or replaced, the technological solution for someone who is unable to eat is a feeding tube. A bypass system of providing nutrition developed for temporary use in intensive care settings in hospitals, a nasogastric tube can be threaded through the nose and down the throat, in patients who cannot swallow due to trauma, unconsciousness, or respiratory failure requiring temporary mechanical ventilation. These tubes also allow use of medications not available in intravenous form. To recover from a reversible stage of an illness or trauma, artificial nutrition is essential, and has been shown to speed healing if the digestive system is intact and the feeding is tolerated by the patient.

Artificial feeding is not completely problem-free. It can cause diarrhea, or reflux up the esophagus (swallowing tube) into the lungs causing aspiration pneumonia. Tolerance of an uncomfortable tube through the nose is not sustainable beyond a couple of weeks due to trauma to the tissues of the nose and throat caused by the friction of the tube itself. If recovery is expected to take weeks or more, a tube is surgically inserted directly into the stomach from the outside wall of the abdomen. Liquid nutrition is then pushed into the tube at intervals with a syringe or by a pump that delivers the food continuously at a programmed rate determined by nutritionist and physician. This feeding technology, designed to sustain a patient through a reversible illness or trauma, has evolved over time into a "default option" to sustain life in the setting of many advanced illnesses that involve a loss of safe swallowing as part of their trajectory. When a feeding tube is chosen by a patient who still has the awareness to choose to live a bit longer than illness would otherwise allow, it can be a tool to give a declining patient enough time to complete important tasks at the end of life—getting financial, emotional, and spiritual houses in order. When a feeding tube is chosen for one who is too ill or unaware of its benefits, such as for a person with advanced dementia, debilitating stroke, severe brain injury, or end-stage neurological disease or cancer, it has the potential not only to increase suffering, but to contribute to a lingering and protracted dying. Not infrequently, the shock of family members on first seeing a tube protruding unnaturally from the belly of someone they love turns to dismay at the dissonance between their good intentions in giving consent for the procedure and their ongoing responsibility in managing its aftermath. The desire, intentions, and repercussions for using life-prolonging therapies such as feeding tubes in terminal illness should be addressed and discussed in family conversations about advance directives long before their use is suggested by a medical team as an option; invariably it is much more emotionally difficult to discontinue a plan of care that includes artificial feeding once it has begun than to decline the option in the first place.

It is not difficult to feel compassion for those who come to a heartbreaking decision to allow a beloved one to die a natural death without interference or prolongation by artificial means, including artificial feeding. It is also not difficult to feel compassion for those who so desire for the beloved to stay with them that they seek extraordinary technological measures to try to make that happen. One of the questions that should be asked in these struggles is the one offered in prayer, "What is the will of God for this person I love, and how would God have me best take care of him or her?"

Our ancestors offered food as sacrifices to God on the temple altars. Manna was the food that became the symbol of God's daily love and protection of the Israelites in the desert. The prayer that Jesus taught his disciples included a petition to "give us this day our daily bread" (Matt. 6:9–15). When Jesus Christ said, "This is my Body" while holding a piece of bread before his disciples on the night before he died (Luke 22:19), he linked forever the act of feeding and eating bread—one of the most basic foods of sustenance—with the sustaining presence of God within ourselves. Is it any wonder that we associate loving with feeding? Is it not also true that when we hold out our hands for the bread of heaven we seek so much more than a bite of bread?

The God who gave us the Bread of Life was giving us the promise of eternal life, not an endless life on earth in our tired, worn-out human bodies. Jesus Christ rose from the dead, conquering the grave, overcoming death. This does not mean that human death is not to continue to be a part of the cycle of human life as it has been since the Creator sent the first people out of the Garden and into the world. Even Lazarus had to die—twice. What would it look like if our last hours, days, and weeks with a loved one could be focused on their comfort, at home, with the time spent in gratitude, and in the work of forgiveness, preparing a way to release them to God, rather than pushing them to eat when their desire to eat is gone? How can we reconcile our need to nourish without sending a suffering body into a wasteland of neither living nor dying? What does it look like when loving people work through all that they believe is expected of them, and move towards a trust in God that allows a holy letting go?

CHAPTER 7

The M Word

Trust in the LORD with all your heart, and do not rely on your own insight. In all your ways acknowledge him, and he will make straight your paths.

PROVERBS 3:5–6

Nick was a lovely gentleman in his mid-eighties who had long suffered from an end-stage lung disease that left him dependent on high-flow oxygen and on other people for just about everything he needed and every move he made. He had rarely been at home in his last year of life, requiring almost constant hospitalization with a very aggressive plan of care to keep him breathing. He frequently needed BiPAP support, in which air is pushed into the airway by a device that includes a tight mask over much of the face. He received repeated bronchoscopy procedures to suction out his airway, in some cases every other day while in the hospital. He did have an advance directive in which stated he did not want to be on a ventilator to keep him alive.

Nick was transferred to a hospice facility under the protest of his daughter, Jean, who had wanted all available aggressive measures continued in spite of their diminishing returns in giving Nick any lasting improvement or quality of life. Nick had a son, but his daughter ran the show. She was a busy executive and traveled frequently, but made it clear to all of her father's medical providers that her goal was to extend her father's life for as long as possible. It was also clear that she loved him very much. It took many difficult conversations for Jean to assent to the DNR order that Nick wanted, and to agree to a plan of care that would potentially include managing Nick's breathlessness with medications, primarily morphine, instead of continuing to send him back to the hospital. She knew that he was too sick to be at home, that even with the private hire nurses he could afford she could not care for him herself, and she could not bear the thought of placing him in a nursing home. Nick's doctors had told her he could not live in the hospital, so Jean allowed him to be transferred to the inpatient hospice facility where registered nurses were on duty 24/7, and then supplemented his care with around-the-clock private duty aides she hired to stay with her father.

Nick slept most of the time but was cheerful and agreeable when awake. He had many visitors who tired him out but clearly doted on him. One night after Nick had had a wonderful day with lots of company, he began to complain that he could not breathe. He was given, according to the medical orders written for symptom management, a small initial dose of morphine. When given in judicious oral doses, morphine has been shown to improve oxygenation and reduce the symptoms of breathlessness without depressing the respiratory drive, as can occur with much larger IV doses. Nick struggled for a while and eventually went to sleep for the rest of the night. His paid caregiver was aware of the symptom and the treatment and did not question it. Though his order for morphine allowed a dose to be given every four hours as needed, there were no further doses given that night or the following day. The next night, however, Nick again became severely short of breath. The nurse caring for him had also been on duty the night before. Nick's breathing rate was rapid and he was anxious. Again the nurse gave Nick a dose of morphine, a little more than she had the night before, both because she knew he had tolerated the initial dose well, and because his symptoms were more severe. She checked on him twice within the hour and found him resting comfortably, asleep; his private hire caregiver was at the bedside. She then went to attend to her other patients. When she went to check on Nick again a couple of hours later, he had died, presumably peacefully in his sleep. His bedside caregiver had not been disturbed by any further signs of distress, nor had she summoned anyone with concerns.

Jean was notified of her father's death and was distraught. On her last visit the previous day he had looked good to her and had been in good spirits, enjoying visitors, and she took this as a sign that he was not dying. She had never accepted from any of Nick's primary or specialty physicians that he did not have much time left; she had not allowed any talk about Nick's impending death from any hospice providers, though that conversation had been attempted many times. Jean's conclusion was that Nick's death been caused by the care he received in the hospice facility. She hired a malpractice attorney, requisitioned his records, and reviewed them with a fine-toothed comb. She filed a formal complaint with the hospice company, wanting the nurse fired for giving Nick the morphine, which she decided had killed her father.

Morphine, an opioid, is a powerful medication that, when used appropriately, can relieve tremendous suffering at end of life, both for patients in terminal decline from primary lung diseases and for those with the lung failure that often accompanies the last hours or days of "active dying." Morphine and other opioids act centrally in the brain to mediate our experience of pain; they also treat breathlessness, ameliorating the feeling of suffocating or drowning. The effectiveness of opioid medications for end-of-life shortness of breath is well documented, and yet it is often the case that no amount of science, experience, or reassurance can disavow a patient, family member, or sometimes even a medical provider, of the fear of them, most particularly of morphine, dubbed "the M word" by hospice and palliative care providers. People who have no qualms about using an opioid that the dentist might prescribe after a dental procedure struggle with explanations of physiologic equivalencies to morphine, and react instead to a culturally imbedded response to its name. Elderly veterans who have experienced combat have told me morphine is something they saw used on the battlefield and since nothing could be *that* bad they wouldn't be needing any morphine, thanks all the same. I have witnessed many cases where fear and anxiety about the use of morphine have led family members to deny that their loved ones were in distress, though the symptoms would be evident to a more objective observer.

Demonstrating safe and appropriate use of morphine, along with aggressive management of its potential side effects of sedation and constipation, is an important task for hospice and palliative care clinicians. Getting patients' and families' trust to actually use morphine or an equivalent opioid to maintain comfort for a loved one is the harder task, one that requires openness, resourcefulness, and a holy patience. The fear of addiction, or of being perceived as addicted, is paramount. There is also the fear of allowing a patient to sleep deeply, because they might not wake up. Many times, the treatment of terminal pain and breathlessness requires acceptance that a disease is progressing, and magical thinking takes over: *If he does not need morphine, then he cannot be that bad, so if I do not give him morphine, he is not that bad.* The conversations to address all of these fears take time, skill, patience. and the willingness of people who are almost overwhelmed with anticipatory grief to sit down and have them; these conversations are often about so much more than morphine.

A series of face-to-face meetings with Jean, her attorney, the hospice CEO, the chief medical director, myself, and others accomplished little other than to allow her to vent her anger and cast a pall of vulnerability over the hospice staff. The hospice medical records were sent to Nick's long-time pulmonologist, who took no issue with his care, saying that Nick's death had long been expected, and that Jean had never been able to accept the impending loss of her father. That we knew she was acting out of grief was little salve for the wounds she created with her threats and accusations. The hospice leadership did some honest evaluation of protocols, and reviewed and narrowed the scope of physician orders for the management of symptoms the nurses were allowed to follow in the inpatient hospice unit, and then waited to see if this would bring Jean some sense of satisfaction. I was torn between my company's directive to hold the necessary boundaries to protect us legally, and my own compulsion to reach out to a daughter who was grieving so deeply and in such a destructive manner. I knew that an attempt to contact her would likely have been seen by her as suspect. This was the most painful learning in Nick's care, that I felt that I had failed his daughter. I had done what I was supposed to do, giving Nick the best care possible, prescribing appropriate medications for his symptoms that allowed him to die as naturally and peacefully as possible. But I had failed Jean—by failing to reach that frightened place inside of her from which she could not let her father go. I had failed to spend enough time with her on her terms, failed to educate her adequately about what Nick's death could look like—with and without morphine for symptom management. I had failed because I saw her as an adversary to Nick's comfort, instead of an ally to be courted in his care.

Most people when questioned about their anxiety about death will say they are not as afraid of death as they are of the suffering they anticipate as part of the dying process. They are afraid of helplessness, sadness, weakness, incontinence, breathlessness, and pain, not necessarily in that order. All of these symptoms can be addressed by loving caregivers and an interdisciplinary team of professionals who have been well trained in best practices, including the use of morphine, to create a plan of care unique to each and all of any one patient's symptoms.

Until a family member or responsible caregiver accepts that someone in their care is dying, it is difficult for them to accept that medications with a proven track record for alleviating symptoms at the end of life should be offered to alleviate suffering that they may or may not acknowledge. In the circumstances where resistance to symptom management is strong, it takes time, challenging conversation, and the building of mutual trust in medical providers to work through long-held fears and misconceptions about the use of morphine and other opioids in end-of-life care. Moving from thinking of morphine as "the M word" to just another manageable tool in the toolbox of care is a painstaking process for some, and an important one that can make the difference between a loved one dying in distress or at peace.

How in the midst of the chaos of caregiving do we find a way to trust in the Lord with all our hearts, relying not on our own insight? Where do we find the courage to trust those who try to make our path a little easier, even when what they offer leaves us skeptical and afraid? How do we live in the tension between protecting one we love from every possible insult, and longing to ease their suffering? How is God working through us and through others in this struggle?

CHAPTER 8

I'm Going Home Tonight

And when he had stepped out of the boat, immediately a man out of the tombs with an unclean spirit met him. He lived among the tombs; and no one could restrain him anymore, even with a chain; for he had often been restrained with shackles and chains, but the chains he wrenched apart, and the shackles he broke in pieces; and no one had the strength to subdue him.

—MARK 5:2–4

Charlie had lived alone for most of his adult life, at least until he was admitted to the hospice inpatient unit after a week's hospitalization, during which he was found to have terminal COPD and lung cancer for which he had refused any disease-directed treatment. He spoke infrequently but walked incessantly. He required oxygen to breathe comfortably but was often found wandering to the ends of the halls toward the outside doors, his oxygen tubing left trailing behind him, abandoned to its green cylindrical tank. His color was ashen, his breathing labored, yet he was determined to make his escape. "I am going home tonight" was his mantra, even as the staff repeatedly tried to coax him back to his room and back onto his oxygen.

We all knew he was dying, even Charlie, and it was heart-breaking not to be able to give a dying man his wish to go home, but Charlie had been found in deplorable condition in his home, in respiratory distress, and metastasis to his brain had stolen the judgment he needed to care for himself, nor would he allow anyone else to come into his home to care for him. He had always been a loner, and had told his social workers that he had spent years "on the road," his euphemism for being homeless. The hospice facility was warm, the staff was kind, and the medications he needed for pain and breathing distress were at the ready for Charlie—but he wanted to go home.

Charlie's mantra cranked up in the last few days of his life. He became adamant, belligerent, especially in the dead of night. He became combative, ready to hit anyone who blocked his way out of the building and though he could not breathe he became crafty, sneaking outside behind a visiting family in order to evade the door alarms, and somehow managing to walk thirty yards into the cold woods behind the building, wearing only a hospital gown over bare feet, before a staff member caught up with him and coaxed him back inside. Eventually Charlie was too weak to get out of bed, and still he cried out to leave. He became calm for brief moments only after receiving small doses of medication for pain and agitation.

Agitation, and its cousins anxiety and delirium, are symptoms frequently encountered in end-of-life care. Anxiety implies fearfulness, a common emotion experienced by many people during illness or its treatment. It can sometimes be addressed with clarity of information, or a comprehensible discussion of diagnosis, treatment, and expected outcomes for a particular medical condition. Patients often express anxiety about the likelihood of experiencing pain, or about how to pay their bills when they cannot work, or about what will happen to their loved ones when they die. Severe anxiety associated with an inability to function or make decisions can require anxiolytic medications.

Delirium describes a temporary loss of orientation to reality; it can be triggered in medical settings by fever, some medications, unfamiliar settings and schedules, a lack of healing sleep, or the experience of anesthesia for surgery. Delirium is treated with gentle reorientation, redirection, evaluation, and adjustment of current medications, and occasionally with symptom-directed medications, when all else fails. For patients with dementia, the inability to process new environments and people can lead to episodes of delirium or a more serious psychosis, such as paranoia, in which their connection with reality is completely lost. People already suffering from dementia do not well tolerate evaluation and treatments for unrelated complex or serious illnesses, and they become agitated. They do not comprehend the need for transport to medical settings, waiting in rooms of unfamiliar people, or invasive procedures such as IV lines, bladder catheters, or tubing blowing oxygen into their nose or mouth.

Agitation describes behaviors like combativeness, yelling, cursing, or disrupting medical treatment by pulling out lines and catheters. Agitation expresses a frustration of the will, a loss of meaningful language to express needs and desires, a lamentation for the irretrievable loss of self-determination.

The term "terminal agitation" belongs to an insider language of those who care for the dying, because though it can look much like anxiety or delirium, it is perceived as a behavior both common and unique to the dying process. Even when a patient has become too weak to walk or even sit, and has even stopped eating and engaging in conversation, agitation can be seen in the form of fidgeting, trying to get out of bed, or reaching for and speaking to someone in the room no one else can see. It can be argued that terminal agitation has physiological triggers such as pain and the body's metabolic derangements during the dying process, which are accelerated by organ failure of liver, kidney, lungs and brain. Yet, terminal agitation can also be largely witnessed as spiritual distress associated with a letting go of life and all of its unfinished business. Many dying patients in my experience have described long-dead loved ones, angels, and even the face of Jesus, whom an elderly woman once told me was right there at the end of her bed "as plain as day." She kept trying to get out of bed to go with him. I struggled to keep her from falling onto a hardwood floor, as she was too weak to even hold a cup in her hand, much less stand. Yet there was something convincing about the way she looked at someone I could not see.

One biblical character that has always come to mind when confronted with a patient suffering from agitation is the man who confronted Jesus in the country of the Gerasenes (Mark 5:1–17). It is understandable that people in ancient times would attribute behaviors of agitation to demonic possession, considering that they blamed all kinds of illness and afflictions on the work of the devil. I believe all humans fear agitation for its wild loss of control, the loss of effective social interaction and communication, and the mirroring of the demons inside each of us that speak to our terror of being alone and unheard, as if ultimately abandoned by God. I have witnessed many people come to this crossroads of isolation and desolation in their dying journeys. When the body is giving up its life force, and the mind is weary and distilling its energy towards the essential, the spirit is moving in a liminal space between self-identity and surrender. Terminal illness leads most people, consciously or unconsciously, to a life review, and those things carried forward to the threshold are guilt, regret, gratitude, love, and grief. Working through the guilt and regret and the grieving of all that will be left behind to come to the peace of gratitude and love may require some agitation. It requires faith enough that God is aware of our suffering and our repentance. It requires hope enough that *all things* are redeemable. Sometimes it requires forgiveness and the release of old pain. Sometimes it requires the presence of one who forgives. Sometimes it is Jacob wrestling with the angel for a blessing before letting go.

Hospice staff tried unsuccessfully to discern what was agitating Charlie. Finally, after much searching on the part of the social worker, a younger sister from whom Charlie had been long estranged found her way to the bedside, and this seemed to calm Charlie considerably. Words of forgiveness and gratitude and love were spoken over the desolation of Charlie's lone-wolf life, and his days of struggle and attempted escapes to "go home tonight" finally gave way to a gentle leaving. Charlie died relaxed and seemingly at peace, not long after his sister's visit.

When Jesus was called out by the unclean spirits inside the man who lived in the tombs—the man who could not be restrained—he sent those same unclean spirits into the swine, off the cliff and into the sea. The witnesses present to this healing then saw the man "clothed and in his right mind." The man begged Jesus to take him with him, but Jesus sent him home instead to his family and friends, to tell of the mercy that had been shown to him.

The fear of not existing is foundational to all other fears. We do not know what we do not know about what happens beyond our last breath on the earth, and it makes us crazy. The fear of the crowd around the demoniac both before and after his healing speaks to this universal fear that is shared even by those with an abiding faith in the presence of God in their day-to-day lives. What we cannot see and cannot hear and cannot control grows larger and more demonic as we approach the end of our world as we know it, and the fear makes us want to growl and howl our way towards the cliff, never truly believing that, unlike the swine, we are meant to fly.

Even as we sit with our own fear and compassion for those we know and love who struggle at the end of life, how can we live each day into the reconciliation of guilt and regret? How can we be clothed in the right mind of forgiveness and gratitude? Where do we see the long unexpected Jesus stepping off of the boat, breaking our chains and bringing healing? Where do we see that great cloud of witnesses waiting and praying for us on our journey home?

CHAPTER 9

I Don't Do Kids

Isaac prayed to the LORD for his wife, because she was barren; and the LORD granted his prayer, and his wife Rebekah conceived. The children struggled together within her; and she said, "If it is to be this way, why do I live?"

—GENESIS 25:21–22(A)

Alicia was born too early, into a world that would be marked by pain and loss. Birth and death were entwined from her beginning as she grew in the womb with her twin. Alicia was the larger and stronger of the two, the beneficiary of a twin-to-twin transfusion that happened long before their birth. Grace lived only a few days. Alicia thrived. Her parents mourned, and then began to make a life for their new infant, both completely innocent and physiologically responsible for her sibling's death.

Alicia was raised like an only child, though she had a grown half-brother who lived away and on his own. She lived with her parents in a beautiful old house on a small farm, next to a pond with overhanging willow trees. The farm had been in her father's family for generations, and the old farmhouse rested in that perpetual state between old charm and new remodeling projects. There were woods to play in nearby, cows, goats, chickens, a dog and at least three cats, and turtles and birds in abundance. Alicia was bright and lively, and liked to help care for the animals, to dance, and to dress up. She was stubborn and opinionated and had an infectious laugh.

Then, when she was six years old, she began to be tired and cranky more than not. She got clumsy, and had a seizure, and then she stepped through the looking glass and became a child with a brain tumor.

Alicia had all and any treatment for her aggressive disease, including surgeries, radiation, and chemotherapies. When those things did not save their child, her parents sought alternative therapies, traveling to a distant state for clinical trials and then for experimental treatments that they brought home and gave her intravenously multiple times a day. They consulted a number of naturalist nutritionists, and fed Alicia with blended shakes of vegetables and supplements, forbidding fast food and ice cream, even as her long use of steroids made her feel like she was starving all the time. They locked the cupboards to keep her from foraging for the peanut butter and jelly and the snacks they ate in secret out in the barn where the adult family and friends huddled to smoke cigarettes and have a beer and a break from Alicia's illness.

By the time hospice was called into Alicia's life, she commanded a space in their home created with a camping pad and lots of colorful pillows on the floor of the kitchen, warmed by a wood stove and the aroma of baking bread. Here she sat cross-legged and leaning against a giant stuffed bear, twice her size and a gift from her uncle, to watch the round-the-clock cartoon station on the TV. Her bald head was covered with a baseball cap, shading her eyes from the light streaming in the windows of the old farmhouse. She could not lie down comfortably because the baseline pressure inside her head had become so great that to surrender her head to gravity would cause her headache pain to grow until she would whine and keen with it.

She rarely slept. She was miserable, and she did not want anything to do with anyone she did not know. Her parents rarely slept. They were miserable, and their grief was like an electric charge in the air, crackling and dangerous. They were continuing to give Alicia infusions of some vitamin and steroid mixture, and resisting her doctors' prognosis of weeks or less based on the progression of Alicia's disease.

We, the hospice team, did what we could—on the one hand so very little, on the other as much as there was room for. We helped the parents to stop the infusions, which were not helping. We persuaded them to treat Alicia's pain, so her headaches would subside long enough for her to sleep for a few hours at a time. We encouraged them to give her what she wanted to eat, chicken nuggets with ketchup and ice cream. No more green liquid concoctions from the blender. And for a week or two, Alicia seemed a little better, and invited us to her floor bed of favorite quilts. We struggled for a bit with constipation, and then with some modest treatment it was better, too. Alicia was able to make it to her church's Christmas play and party and came home with a basket full of candy. She did not want it for herself, but delighted in giving it away to anyone who walked in the door. It was lovely to see her happiness, and sad to know it would be transient. She felt better, but she was not getting better.

Alicia died a day or two after she had been coaxed from the floor into a hospital bed, fascinated by the automatic controls she could operate to raise and lower the head, the foot, and the entire bed. The bed had been set up in the breakfast nook, where she could look out the windows on three sides to Christmas lights on the barn and the birdfeeders just outside the window. The table had been moved to make room for the bed but the built-in benches made a place for family and friends to keep vigil at her bedside. As a quiet snow fell outside, Alicia's pain had returned with a vengeance, and a new reluctance to increase her pain medications was causing friction between her parents. She sat up on the side of the bed, legs under and arms and torso leaning over the bedrails, refusing to lie back even with the head of the bed raised all the way, though she appeared to be exhausted. Her lungs became wet and congested. Her color was ashen as she fought wearing oxygen with the last of her strength.

Alicia was dying, and she had crossed the impossible threshold where her suffering was worse than her dying. I could hear her parents' prayers, though they were silent: her father praying, "Take me instead," and her mother praying, "Take her and make the suffering stop." Alicia's breathing had the rattling sound that told us there would not be much time left. She was mumbling, but clearly asked for root beer. Her mother's face contorted in horror, thinking it would surely drown her, but she wanted it, so I lifted a thimbleful in a tiny cup to cracking lips and she drank it. When I told her to sip slowly, reflexively cautious about the possibility she might aspirate it, she said, with no little contempt, "I am not stupid." She was six, and dying, and she was right: she was not stupid and knew what was happening, and she was not nearly as anxious about it as everyone else in the room. After she chased her last dose of pain medication with root beer, she told us, "I'm done," and she finally lay down, and her mother lay beside her, crooning softly and cradling her head; her baseball cap had been traded for a soft knit one of blues and greens. Once everyone in the house was quiet, I left, knowing today would be the day that Alicia would go. The nurse stayed with the family and I drove towards my next appointment. Knowing I was already late, I pulled into a snow-covered church parking lot and went into the empty church. In the quiet I prayed for Alicia's suffering to be over. It was not my prayer to pray, and I prayed it with all my heart. In less than an hour, the nurse called to tell me that she was gone.

I drove back to the house, and watched as the nurse helped Alicia's mother bathe her and dress her in her favorite pajamas, clean and still warm from the dryer. When the men from the funeral home arrived, Alicia's father carried her body in his arms and placed her on the stretcher, where the men covered her with blankets and carried her gently and quietly away in the falling snow.

There is nothing more broken in my experience than a world in which a child has died. If it is true, as Hemingway wrote, that we are diminished by each death of another, then we are reduced to rubble at the death of a child. And if anything can strike cold terror into the heart of an experienced hospice professional, it's the kids. Usually with little notice or chance to prepare for it emotionally or spiritually, the news that "we're getting a kid" moves through a hospice team like a palpable weighted fog.

An early response is "I hope not." This first phase of denial comes knowing that children seldom enter hospice care because parents often change their minds and choose for their dying child to stay in the hospital, where they have come to know and depend on longstanding relationships with their acute care teams. The dread for hospice workers in assuming the care of a dying child comes from the understanding that dying children have complex physical needs requiring specialized and seldom-used skills; more than that, witnessing the pain of a parent losing a child is almost too much to bear. A child who enters hospice care is usually close to death from some long and terrible experience that has included many prolonged hospitalizations, procedures, surgeries, trips to the most special of specialists at famous clinics in distant states. Many of them have been ferried around by Angel Flights—to far-away specialty clinics or hospitals, and by Make-A-Wish—to Disney World and Legoland, searching for both the miracle cure and the memories of a lifetime to hedge the bet. By the time the child's primary medical team begins the work of persuading a family that there are no more treatments available to save their child, that they are not to be one of the "lucky ones," the plan of care to sustain that child's life is already likely to include artificial feeding and hydration, central lines and tubes, oxygen, and sometimes even home ventilators. The child would not have had any semblance of normal life in a long time. He would not have been to school, to a playground, to soccer practice, or to a movie theater in ages. She would be weak and frail, and often fractious, and sometimes in pain that parents were reluctant to acknowledge or treat. For children with chronic medical conditions or severe developmental delay with neurological impairment, sometimes since birth or infancy, there might have been a paid nurse in the home for years to assist with complex care needs who has developed a strong surrogate emotional attachment. Like an appendage family member, an outside agency nurse could display a complex assortment of anxieties, including anticipatory grief for a child she has come to love, pending loss of employment, and territorial resistance to allowing an outsider—a hospice nurse—to learn the care needs of "her" child.

To accomplish the shift from doing everything possible to keep a child alive, to doing everything possible to keep a child comfortable while foregoing life-prolonging treatment, is an impossible task for parents, grandparents, extended family members, and long-time professional caregivers. The natural order of life is altered when children die, and resistance to this shift is powerful from all quarters. By this time in a painful trajectory of illness, a child would likely be known in hundreds of e-mail and Facebook prayer chains, have possibly been honored with a community fundraiser, and lived in a family that has been completely restructured around that child's illness and needs. Siblings are largely on their own by this time, being kept in the dark about what is coming, receiving care from grandparents, cousins, or friends who have been doing the best they could, and estranged from their dying sister or brother, who has sucked up all the energy in every room and still gotten a Make-A-Wish trip.

Parents, if married to each other, are often by this time struggling to be a couple, as one has stayed in the world of work to maintain health insurance and pay the mortgage or rent, while the other has long withdrawn from the world to become a full-time nurse and champion, investing 24/7 attention and effort into keeping the child as well and as happy as possible. Each role carries guilt and blame. If divorce and/or remarriage preceded the illness of the child, the usual negotiations of blended families and the true affections of step-parents have added to the chaos and complexity. The family dysfunction around a dying child becomes embedded within an insurmountable wall of grief, and walking into that space feels like David meeting Goliath, or Daniel that lion.

It is no wonder that even some seasoned hospice workers "don't do kids." If a hospice employer is able and willing to respect this preference, and if fellow employees are willing to allow some grace for those who might have a child the same age or who have no pediatric experience, the work with children is left to a few. It has always been with fear and trepidation, and an awareness of all of these complications, that I have witnessed brave nurses be the first to knock on the door of a home with a dying child inside. Prepared to be unwelcome and bearing the responsibility of "bringing death into the house," they go in anyway, because they were called to, and because someone has to. And I, the doctor, have followed.

Though terminal illness in children is statistically rare, I have been the hospice doctor for too many children. Any one of them was too many. All of them have left memories like scars, even those who had very little need of me in my role, because of a long-standing and faithful relationship between the family and the child's oncologist or other pediatric specialist. I understood that I represented a shadow side of medicine to people, and recognized that I was invited into the homes of the dying primarily for my skills and my fearlessness in symptom management—to help control pain or breathlessness or constipation—often accepted only after the reassurance of the trusted physician who invited me and my hospice team into the sheltered space around the child and family.

More often than not, my suggestions were resisted and rejected, because of the cultural fear of pain medications, and because of the fears in any particular family that to acknowledge pain and discomfort in the child meant to acknowledge that the disease causing those symptoms was progressing unchecked. To admit to the presence of pain that required treatment was to admit that death was approaching. To deny that pain was present kept death at bay; the burden of this magical thinking often fell upon the child in pain. It was not uncommon to see two parents taking opposing views on treating their child's distressing symptoms. One wanted the child comfortable at all costs. The other wanted the child at all costs.

For one who believes in a God of mercy, being involved in the care of a dying child feels like a slip and fall into a deep, dark hole. The first question of vocal doubters is always, "How can you believe in a loving God who allows a child to suffer and die?" It is never a question I want to address, because there is really no answer that satisfies the one who asks the question. All I can do is remember what I have witnessed and pray a lament, not for the children who are no longer suffering, but for those who loved them, whose lives were forever altered by losing them. I can tell those parts of their stories that opened up the thin spaces between this world and another, where I knew the presence of God in the midst of the suffering.

There are too many stories in the Bible about parents and children for this not to be an important touchstone between God and humanity. The stories of desperate love and loss of children begin with our first mother, Eve, as she endured the death of her son Abel at the hand of her son Cain (Gen 4:1–16).

A covenant relationship between God and Abraham involved a willingness to sacrifice Isaac, the beloved and promised child of his old age, casting a shadow over a promise to be given descendants as numerous as the stars (Gen. 22:1–19). The suffering of Hagar and her son Ishmael was rooted in the impatient desperation of Sarah to have a child, even outside of her barrenness (Gen. 21:8–10). When Abraham sent Hagar into the desert with her child to die, she gave the boy the last of the water and tried to shade him with her own parched body as she prayed to God for deliverance (Gen. 21:14–20).

Rachel wanted to die herself for the unfulfilled desire of a child (Gen. 30:1) and Jacob, though he had been blessed with a dozen sons by four different mothers, said, "I am the one you have bereaved of children: Joseph is no more, and Simeon is no more, and now you would take Benjamin. All this has happened to me!" (Gen. 42:36).

The mother of Moses hid her young infant in the reeds and rushes of the river to save him from the infanticide of Pharaoh, and then surely heard the cries of other parents trying to fight off soldiers sent to kill their baby boys who could not be hidden (Exod. 2:1–10). Hannah sang to God for the gift of Samuel after a long season of barrenness, and then she gave the child back to God by giving him to the priest Eli when he was weaned (1 Sam. 1).

David wept over his dying infant born of Bathsheba, and continued to weep later in his life over the multiple tragedies that befell his children: "O my son Absalom, my son, my son Absalom! Would that I had died instead of you, O Absalom, my son, my son!" (2 Sam. 18:33)

Jesus prayed over and blessed children and told the adults around them that it was to children that the kingdom of heaven belonged, because it was children who knew how to enter (Luke 18:15–17).

The ultimate suffering parent was Mary, a mother who was willing to carry a child whose very presence in her womb brought shame to her and her betrothed, Joseph, and then to give birth to him in a shelter for animals; a mother who watched her son leave home for a wanderer's life—challenging authority and making outrageous claims; a mother who saw the gift of healing come from her own child's hands, and then saw her child harassed, arrested, tortured and killed, and finally lowered into her arms at the foot of a cross because of that gift. How did she do it? How did she bear it?

The only way I can try to answer that question is in another story. My part in it was small, yet its power in my life was large. Baby Morgan was born the first child to lovely young parents who had made a life together and prepared a loving space in that life for him. He came into the world with a genetic disorder, a chromosomal abnormality that was a random mutation; neither parent could claim the guilt of being a carrier of potential disaster for their child. They had known before his birth that Morgan would not be "normal." They had received all judicious prenatal care and special genetic counseling when routine tests led to more specialized ones, and scans of him in the womb had revealed that all was not well. They had been prepared by their medical team that Morgan might die in his first day of life, and that if he did not, he might live only weeks to months; that his brain would never develop enough to allow him to walk, talk, or understand what was happening around him. They knew he would have special needs, would have difficulty with breathing, and with feeding, and that he would require exquisite care.

Both of Morgan's parents were young professionals; they had just bought an old house in the country that they had planned to fix up over time for what they hoped would be a growing family. They had a strong faith in God and a supportive church community. Neither of them had ever cared for an infant, and there were no grandparents, aunts, uncles, or siblings nearby. They had approached the birth cautiously, and had gathered minimal equipment and supplies at their home, because they knew that Morgan might never go home with them—that he might die in his first hours or days of life. And then he didn't.

Less than five pounds at birth, Morgan was pale with almost translucent skin, long thin fingers, a tiny mouth, and piercing very dark eyes; it was unclear how much he could see. He had wispy strands of hair, usually covered with a cap to keep him warm. Anyone who looked at Morgan could see that something was "wrong" with him. But he was perfect in God's eyes.

Morgan's parents elected to bring him home with hospice services when he was a few weeks old, because even though he did not die shortly after birth, he was not expected to live very long. He had been found to have the complication of a heart defect, but was too frail to undergo corrective surgery, and his parents did not want him to suffer through an invasive surgery and its aftermath when his life expectancy was so short. Morgan was breathless with any exertion, even with his soundless crying, and was dependent on oxygen through a tiny nasal cannula. He was fed through an even tinier tube threaded through his nose, back down his throat to his stomach. He did not have the coordination or the energy to swallow enough pumped breast milk to sustain him, so his parents had learned to give him very small feedings through the tube, precisely timed every two hours around the clock; at the same time they allowed him to suck for pleasure, and over a few weeks he began to swallow a teaspoon or two on his own. They also learned to rethread the tube and get it in the right place if Morgan managed to dislodge it with those long fingers of his, even though it was secured to his tiny cheek with tape.

Kelly was the hospice nurse who stepped into Morgan's life; she was young and single, and had never been a parent. She was a generous soul and would do anything for her patients. She had a deep grounding faith in God and a very sunny disposition. She fell in love with Morgan and his parents at first sight, knowing they would all break her heart. Even without much pediatric experience, she took on Morgan's needs, and found people to teach her what she did not know to be a good nurse to Morgan and his little family. She threw out the boundaries of professional care, gave them her cell phone number, and was ready to be personally available anytime—even nights and weekends that were covered by an after-hours staff. Morgan's mom and dad learned to trust Kelly, and looked forward to her visits, her recommendations, and her reassuring smile. We often made visits together, for mutual support, as she depended on my physical assessments and I depended on her procedural skills to give this child and family whatever we had to offer. I would sit in my car before visits, praying for courage, and after visits I would drive down the road, park my car, and sit for a while before going to visit anyone else.

Morgan's father was devoted to him; he learned all of his care, and could help with rethreading his feeding tube, setting up the pump, and gently changing diapers and clothes. But eventually he had to go back to work, which involved a time-consuming commute, having already taken weeks off after the birth. Morgan's mother took an extended leave from her job, and set herself to being the best mother she could be for as long as she would be given the task. She rarely put Morgan down, usually only in his raised infant seat after feedings to help control his reflux.

One bright sunny day during one of our visits, we found Morgan's mom sitting on their sofa with Morgan lying next to her on his back, looking mesmerized at the light dancing across a picture window behind them. The show was made up of the wind in the tall trees in the woods behind their house; the sun sparkled through the moving leaves, and Morgan was captivated. It was the one place, other than sleeping in his mother's arms, where Morgan looked comfortable, where his tiny face was not expressing anxiety or discomfort.

Morgan's mother calmly told us that Morgan was talking to God. Her comment startled me, but not Kelly, and not by its content, but by the peace with which it was spoken; I asked her to tell me more. She said with heartfelt authority that Morgan belonged to God, and that she and her husband had known this from before he was born, before they knew that Morgan would not be a healthy child destined for a long life. They saw their call as his parents to be his caregivers in his short life, and to learn what he could teach them about God's love, sharing that with others. It was their job to make him as happy and comfortable as possible, and then when God called him home, to let him go. They were sad, already grieving so much, and yet they were faithful believers that God was present with them in this journey. Watching God talking to Morgan in the dancing of the light and their relationship with Kelly, whom they saw as exactly the right person to be on this journey with them and with Morgan, was confirmation.

I almost stopped breathing. It almost makes me stop breathing to remember it. My first unspoken question was, "What kind of church do you go to?" My second was, "How does someone so young and tender have so much wisdom and grace?" My own anxiety about caring for this special child began to dissipate. My fear at failing these loving and generous parents was taken away into the trees. The lament of loss was taken into the arms of a God who longs to gather together the children of Jerusalem as a hen gathers her brood under her wings (Matt. 23:37).

Morgan's parents were faithful to their call. With Kelly's patient guidance they carefully considered each decision about his care, always leaning to consideration of Morgan's comfort. When he became distressed after feedings, they cut them back and gave less more often, sleeping in turns, and rarely. Kelly ordered them an adult hospital bed, so that they could lie down beside Morgan with his little body on a raised incline, allowing him to breathe, and allowing his parents to rest their arms from holding him upright while still cradling him.

When Morgan died, they were not ready, but they were faithful, and Kelly was with them. Their deep sorrow was mixed with exhaustion, and relief that Morgan's suffering was over. They spoke at his funeral service of being surrounded by God's love, touching them in profound ways through Morgan's short and beautiful life. Though his body was gone, and offered to science in an ultimate sacrifice to others through what could be learned from his genetic imperfection, Morgan was with them always and ever after, in the light that danced through the trees and through their window.

How is it possible that losing a child is survivable for a loving parent? How did we come to believe that though God has given us the responsibility to love and care for them, that children belong to us as possessions? Where is the biblical promise that our children will outlive us, and that keeping them safe and healthy is something we can do without God? What kind of faith does it take to be so grounded in the will of God that we might love a child the way Morgan's parents did? What kind of faith does it take to let a child go and trust that child to God?

CHAPTER 10

Not Dead Yet

While he was still speaking, someone came from the leader's house to say, "Your daughter is dead; do not trouble the teacher any longer." When Jesus heard this, he replied, "Do not fear. Only believe, and she will be saved." When he came to the house, he did not allow anyone to enter with him, except Peter, John, and James, and the child's father and mother. They were all weeping and wailing for her; but he said, "Do not weep; for she is not dead but sleeping." And they laughed at him, knowing that she was dead. But he took her by the hand and called out, "Child, get up!" Her spirit returned, and she got up at once. Then he directed them to give her something to eat. Her parents were astounded; but he ordered them to tell no one what had happened.

—LUKE 8:49–56

The first time I took a CPR (cardiopulmonary resuscitation) class was during my pre-medical education, unsure if I would even be accepted at medical school. I worked in a children's hospital on weekends as a phlebotomist, drawing blood from tiny fingers and heels, and was required to take a CPR class. It certified me to determine if someone who was unresponsive had a pulse, and to begin rescue breathing and chest compressions while calling for a higher level of help. One week after taking this class, on a quiet Saturday morning when only one lab tech and I were working a twelve-hour shift, Jonathan, a ten-year-old with a genetic metabolic disorder and a fever, came in for some lab work ordered by his private physician. He was listless and looked very sick. The hospital did not have an emergency room at the time, and there was no doctor on duty with any responsibility to care for this child. We were unsuccessful at reaching his attending doctor by phone, and I began to page the resident on call for inpatients to come down to see him. Jonathan could barely hold his eyes open and did not flinch or protest at having his blood drawn; he was really sick. With some protest, the resident said he would come down when he got a chance but was very busy upstairs. There were no cots in the lab as we generally only drew blood on the wards, so I told the child's father he could lie him down on the x-ray table across the hall. As the lab technician and I were preparing for our morning rounds we heard him calling out that his child was not breathing.

Terrified, I ran to see a child turning gray from not breathing. I screamed for the med tech to call a code. It took a while for the operator to understand and to communicate that the emergency was in the x-ray department on a Saturday. I climbed up onto the high table, leaned over the child and began rescue breathing. The tech behind me began chest compressions. It seemed like an eternity until upstairs nursing staff, medical residents, and an attending physician making weekend rounds showed up and took over. The child was intubated and taken to ICU to be admitted—with a pulse.

In shock at what had just happened on a quiet, ordinary Saturday morning, I went to the small lab bathroom, sat down, locked the door, and shook for a long time. I don't remember if I was crying, but I do remember being angry—at the parent who did not take the child to a real emergency room, at the physician who had sent such a sick child into the lab, at the resident who would not come when I called him, and at the world that could make children so sick and vulnerable. At the time, I was not generally on speaking terms with God. On the following Monday, I was called by the hospital medical director to tell me that the child tested positive for strep. Because I had done mouth-to-mouth rescue breathing I should pick up a course of antibiotics for myself. I was encouraged to visit the child in the hospital and I did. He was sitting up in his bed, pale but smiling, coloring, with no memory of the trauma of Saturday. His father at his bedside expressed gratitude for what I had done for his child. I was stunned that he had lived, and that he had recovered, that it worked. I became a believer in CPR, and that I might someday be a doctor.

A few years later, when I was a third-year medical student learning to make my way in the world of a teaching hospital, everything was simultaneously exciting, terrifying, and exhausting. Medical students were expected to be attentive, respectful of the hierarchy of authority (intern, resident, chief resident, attending physician), knowledgeable, and ever prepared to function in the next new situation that presented itself. The most challenging was a Code Blue. The overhead call of *Code Blue* and its location, announcing that someone in this hospital had no pulse and had stopped breathing, that someone had *died* and presumably wanted to be brought back from the dead, was broadcast in the familiar voice of the hospital operator at the same time multiple pagers began screaming, summoning each one on that hierarchical list.

The first Code Blue called in my first week of clinical rotations brought my team of four brand new medical students to a room already crowded with a large red "code cart," monitors, nurses, respiratory therapists, and doctors. Family members and visitors were shoved out into the hall. Another student and I sneaked around the crowd to the inside corner at the head of the bed, and our attending, a young chief resident in internal medicine, told us to watch and stay out of the way.

The patient, Marie, was a woman whose age was difficult to determine, because her entire body was covered by skin that was bright red, blistered, and peeling. She had been suffering, and dying, from a rare allergic reaction to a common medication that caused the layers of her skin and her mucosal tissues to separate and slough away from each other and deteriorate. Toxic epidermal necrolysis, or TEN, begins as a simple itchy rash, and progresses over days to a condition similar to being scalded, inside and out. At that time, in the early 1980s, it was not considered survivable; today these patients are managed in specialized burn units and still the mortality for the condition is very high.

Her eyes were closed to the frenzied and almost violent activity that involved her body. One person was kneeling on the edge of the bed, leaning over her and pushing both hands into her chest with rhythmic force. Another was standing over the head of her bed, holding her jaws open with a lighted instrument to see down her throat, trying to insert a tube between her vocal cords, so that oxygen-enriched air could be pushed through a bag into her airway with enough force and volume to inflate her lungs. Others were tearing into boxes and wrappers from the code cart for intravenous drugs designed to jump-start the electrical impulses of her heart. We all jumped back while holding up our hands, as in a choreographed dance, at the loud command to "CLEAR" as the defibrillator paddles were placed on her chest in two places, releasing a shock that made her body jump on the bed, multiple times.

All third-year medical students had recently attended a CPR refresher course. We would not take the ACLS (advanced cardiac life support) course until we were interns. We were not invited to participate "hands on," and we were too low on the medical care hierarchy to prescribe and administer drugs, though we were expected to know what they were and what they were intended to do. All the training, however, did not prepare us for the drama—the commando orders of the physician in charge, the assault of so many hands on a lifeless body, the flow of adrenalin in the room—and not just what was being pushed artificially into the patient. I witnessed wonder and horror at the same time, that this human being's moment of death was being hijacked in a carefully orchestrated performance that brought together training and technology and helplessness and hubris and good intentions—none of which was able to bring Marie back to life. When the code was "called," announcing a time of death (the time at which there was a general consensus in the room that the resuscitation did not work), people filed out of the room, leaving me and my fellow medical students in the far corner the last to be able to leave.

As we slid past the bed for the door, I noticed that the cardiac monitor from the code cart was still on, showing a normal sinus rhythm on the screen. I pointed it out to my fellow doctor-to-be and we both raced into the hall to announce that she was "not dead yet." About half of the original team came back in looking for a Lazarus-like miracle, and resumed the resuscitation protocol until they realized the patient still had no pulse, and that the blips on the screen were being driven by an epinephrine drip that had not been disconnected from the patient. A chemical message feeding an electrical impulse was being received somewhere, but the heart could no longer translate that message into the pumping action that was necessary for life. She was gone. She had really died. The monitor was turned off, the drip disconnected, and everyone left the room again.

I was upset after witnessing this experience, embarrassed at causing the awkward re-entry of the code team by misunderstanding the apparently normal rhythm on the monitor, and because Marie had suffered so much, and had died anyway. My feelings were compounded after a discussion with our attending physician while de-briefing the code. He thought he was being reassuring when he told us that the patient never had a chance of surviving anyway, that her condition was fatal.

I asked him why we went through the whole exercise of resuscitation if they knew she would not benefit. He said that it was done for *us* to learn—to have the experience, to go through the motions to further our training. It was then that I wanted to be sick, feeling the bile rise up to the back of my throat. I had watched an assault on a human being at the moment of her leaving this life intended to make me a better doctor, to give me tools that might be used down the road to save someone else. It was then that I understood that belief in the power of medicine, even in the power of resuscitation, was complicated.

Since those early days, an attempt at resuscitation of a person who stops breathing, or whose heart stops beating—in a medical setting or in the community—has evolved to consider the possibility of personal choice. To resuscitate is always the default option for any rescue or medical personnel who might be present, an ethical obligation to act; yet there is also an ethical obligation to inquire about an *advance directive*, a legal document stating an individual's considered preferences regarding resuscitation and its components: chest compressions and rescue breathing; electrical shocks using a defibrillator; intubation and mechanical ventilation; and drugs designed to reboot a heart beating too fast, too slow, or not at all. In my professional lifetime, there has been some cultural evolution towards possible choices about how we might die. We are not usually given the choice of whether we acquire a terminal condition that hastens our death, or whether we become victims of accident or disaster. Yet if we make the effort to become educated about our choices and what they mean, we *can* have a say as to what our final days and hours might look like, whether we want to leave this world in a resuscitation drama, or to request a physician's order for DNR (do not resuscitate), DNAR (do not attempt resuscitation), or AND (allow natural death).

When a person is making preparations for death, creating an advance directive for health care can be just as important as a last will and testament. An advance directive can take many forms. The ones offered in an attorney's office can be blanketed with legal jargon that requires some interpretation; they are centered on choosing and naming an *agent* to speak and act for you when you cannot speak and act for yourself. "Five Wishes"[1] is a widely-distributed user-friendly option that is accepted in most states; it goes through a series of questions about many things (beyond CPR) regarding individual preferences at end of life: Do you like a lot of people around or do you like more quiet?

1. "Five Wishes," Aging with Dignity, *https://agingwithdignity.org/five-wishes/about-five-wishes*.

Do you want music playing and what kind? It is designed to create conversations with family and friends, so that the agent you choose to make any needed decisions for you actually *knows* your preferences ahead of time and is therefore able to make decisions you might make for yourself if you could.

Some people attend to these things when of sound body and mind, perhaps because they are planners and want some future control over possible situations of helplessness as end of life approaches. Others complete their legal documents, including wills, only when death is breathing down their necks. Some people never do this, and the decision to resuscitate or not is made in the last hours or days of life after a difficult conversation with a doctor who takes the time to explain it all to a patient, family, or friend—that a body is failing, and that all medical opportunities and options to help it have already been exhausted, save those to prepare for and secure a peaceful and painless death.

These conversations are difficult and take a long time if done well. They are filled with anxiety, and grief, and guilt, and sadness. If the DNR is chosen, then patient and family begin to prepare themselves for the letting go, and whatever that means within their family or system of belief about death and what comes after. It can be a time of prayer, and hopefully for expressions of forgiveness and gratitude. For some, it is a time of reconnecting with God; for others a time for friends and more distant family to rally around for support.

Some patients and their families will never choose a DNR order, even when death is imminent. They want every kind of life support medical science has to offer at any cost—ventilators to breathe for the patient, supported if necessary by tracheotomies—a hole cut in the throat to connect the breathing tube. They opt for surgically implanted feeding tubes, heart bypass machines, dialysis, drips of medications to make the heart beat—anything and everything designed to prolong life by shoring up multiple organ systems regardless of the prospects of recovery to a meaningful or productive life. Sometimes this push to sustain a technology-dependent life is undertaken for a temporary and very personal reason—to allow loved ones to travel to the bedside to say goodbye or to allow an opportunity to emotionally prepare for a coming death.

Sometimes a demand for resuscitation comes out of a fear of death, even in one who has been known to have lived a good life with a strong professed faith in God. Patients and families hold out, even within days or hours of impending death, hoping for a miracle. They believe if they accede to the possibility of death, that God will perceive them as not faithful enough to receive the miraculous healing they desire and pray for. The refusal to allow withdrawal of life support permitting a natural death can be enmeshed with guilt, unfinished business with the patient, or as in one case I was involved with, a fear that because the patient had not lived a holy life, allowing his death to happen would have been a "sentence to hell," for which his relative did not want responsibility.

The health care system in America honors an ethic of individual autonomy and personal and religious choice above many other things—including scientific evidence and the collective resources of a society. All of those resources that can be brought to bear to keep a failing body alive cannot always make it well, and this can lead to a kind of living death, whose last gasp is postponed through a land of suffering with a cost beyond its monetary value. At this stage of critical and terminal illness, health care is continued, regardless of the patient's ability to pay for it, regardless of insurance. Decisions are never made in critical care based on ability to pay. Once a patient makes his or her way into critical care in an ICU, unless an advance directive states otherwise, the attitude is "full court press" to sustain life— or any semblance thereof. More recent efforts by the relatively new specialty of palliative care or a locally strong hospital ethics committee are applied within a culture of resistance to "giving up" too soon. Even strong training of doctors in end-of-life issues and good communications skills cannot overcome an underlying and ultimate goal to save lives. These competing values underlie messages from medical professionals that can be mixed and confusing to patients and families under stress from critical illness.

Initially, the only message communicated in medical care is, "We can fix anything and we want to help you." When none of the fixes works well enough and the patient is reduced to a dependence on a sophisticated technology for a poor quality of life and no hope of recovery, then the non-verbal message can be one of abandonment. Families feel abandoned by the medical team who can no longer offer hope of recovery. The medical team suffers from the demoralizing experience of going through the motions of care for a patient they know will die in spite of their best efforts. The patient is often abandoned as family members and friends drift away from the twenty-four-hour waiting room vigils, go back to work and their lives, leaving an unresponsive family member on life support systems to be cared for by "professionals." Conversations about failure to cure or preparation for death, especially if they are unskilled, can become contentious and cause emotional distress for everyone involved.

This scenario of impasse is familiar to many who have experienced the death of a loved one. It leaves a trail of complicated grief, colored with confusion and resentment. It speaks of lost opportunities for accomplishing tasks necessary for a peaceful death—expressions of gratitude, forgiveness, and love. Most people, when asked, say they would want a peaceful death, at home, not "on machines." Few people, however, are prepared to do what is necessary to make this happen, because though we know in our minds that all of us must die, in our hearts we do not believe that dying applies to ourselves or those we love anytime soon, or ever, really. We think that talking about death and preparing our advance directives will bring it on, so we whistle past the graveyard and put it off another day. This can leave those who care about us unexpectedly holding a bag of what feels like life and death decisions when we do decline and approach death. In reality these decisions are not between life and death, but between one kind of death and another.

One little-known and often-ignored consequence of resuscitation (until it's too late) is the return of a beating heart without recovery of a functioning brain. The odds of surviving an out-of-hospital cardiopulmonary arrest with attempted resuscitation long enough to get to the hospital (even for a patient who is not already suffering with a terminal illness) are around 26 percent; the probability of surviving that hospitalization to discharge are around 9 percent.[2]

---

2. Bryan McNally, MD, et al., "Out-of-Hospital Cardiac Arrest Surveillance: Cardiac Arrest Registry to Enhance Survival (CARES), United States, October 1, 2005–December 31, 2010," Centers for Disease Control Morbidity and Mortality Weekly Report: Surveillance Summaries (2011) 60 (SS08); 1–19, http://www.cdc.gov/mmwr/preview/mmwrhtml/ss6008a1.htm.

The odds of surviving an in-hospital arrest to discharge are around 17 percent or less, with half of these returning home and the other half to some kind of nursing or rehab facility. Of this small number of survivors, the rate of cancer patients' survival after CPR has been found to be less than 7 percent, and if they were in ICU, less than 3 percent. Data from 2003 has shown that only 2% of patients on dialysis live 6 months after CPR.[3] This illustrates what many people in health care have experienced—that for a patient who is suffering from terminal illness, CPR can be an exercise in futility that does not bring people back to meaningful life, but if successful, only prolongs an inevitable death for a short time, often escalating the care needed for that patient such that it becomes impossible for him or her to leave the ICU or other setting of profound dependence until death occurs again. This information is not always shared with those trying to make a decision about CPR; sometimes when the information *is* available, odds of two to seven percent begin to sound good to those who are desperate to avoid death. They think, *someone* has to be in the two- to seven-percent range, so why not me, or my loved one?

Where is God in this conversation and in this decision? Some people say that only God decides the moment of death and it is our responsibility as humans to resist that moment with everything we have to throw at it. Only then should death be accepted. Others say that all of our technology is just a contemporary version of that apple in the Garden of Eden—that the knowledge and technology we acquire and use to hold back

3. David Ramenofsky, MD, and David E. Weissman, MD, Palliative Care Network of Wisconsin, "Fast Facts and Concepts #179: CPR Survival in the Hospital Setting," revised July 2015, *http://www.mypcnow.org/#!blank/lb6ty*.

death challenges God, and that "playing God" brings more suffering into our dying than was ever intended by our Creator. Some agree that our death-defying culture is not a good thing—until we need it to come to the aid of ourselves, or those we love.

How can we speak of these things in a way that feels safe and reduces our fear and anxiety about dying? Why do we rarely hear these conversations in church? What are the stories in our Christian tradition that give us pause to question our usual assumptions about dying and death? Did Jesus weep because his friend Lazarus had died, or because he knew that for Jesus to be glorified, Lazarus would have to live with the consequences of the miracle of his return to life, and someday have to die again? Why did Jesus tell the parents of the restored little girl to tell no one? In what ways can we learn to grow in our trust in God that we do not fear meeting him face to face?

CHAPTER 11

I'm Not Ready Yet

> Lord, let me know my end and the number of my days,
>   so that I may know how short my life is.
> You have given me a mere handful of days,
> and my lifetime is nothing in your sight;
>   truly, even those who stand erect are but a puff of wind.
>   —Psalm 39:5–6 BCP

Connor was a young father in his forties. He had two boys in high school and had been divorced from their mother since the boys were very young. Living in the same community, the parents had worked out joint custody arrangements that had the children living with each parent for half the time, negotiating shared holidays. During the time Connor had been recovering from the trauma of his divorce, he began attending a church that was loving and supportive. He rebuilt a life, and after a few years met and married a young woman with whom he was able to share his faith and his strong commitment to his children. She grew to love Connor's sons and her role as a stepmother.

Shortly after their wedding and honeymoon, Connor began to have symptoms of abdominal pain that did not respond to the usual treatments for reflux. He was diagnosed with cancer in his esophagus and began a year of arduous surgeries, chemotherapies, and nutritional therapies that consumed his family's life. Connor lost weight and became extremely gaunt. He tried to work for a while but eventually had to assume a "disability" and stay home. He saved his energy and attention for his children's time in his home, but meeting their day-to-day needs began to fall to their stepmother.

By the time hospice care was recommended for Connor, he had outlived the prognosis given by multiple physician specialists. He had received all the treatment anyone had suggested, including clinical trials. Most of his esophagus and stomach had been removed and the cancer had involved his liver and his lungs. He had been unable to eat enough to sustain himself for almost a year, and had been living on TPN (total parenteral nutrition) through a central IV port implanted into his chest. This form of liquid intravenous nutrition is designed for short term use—days to weeks—when the digestive tract that has been damaged by surgery, infection, or trauma cannot absorb nutrients and only until such healing takes place to allow the patient to tolerate oral or tube feedings. Connor had lost any chance of that kind of recovery, but because of his age and tolerance of the TPN, it was continued indefinitely to sustain him for as long as his cancer would allow him to live.

Connor was a genuinely nice guy. His cancer had not made him bitter; he was grateful for his church family and his friends, and for his new wife who had barely gotten to know him when he was healthy. He spoke openly of his Christian faith and was not afraid to die, but he was not ready to leave his children. Connor entered a phase of his life that was a "new normal"; he spent his days in a recliner, looking out the window or at television, taking journeys to the bathroom, and wetting his mouth with ice chips and spitting out the melted water. If he tried to swallow any pills or food, he would vomit shortly after, so he stopped trying. He had considerable pain, and when trans-dermal pain medication delivered by patches began to lose its effectiveness, hospice provided a PCA (patient controlled analgesia) pump. Through this device managed by the hospice nurse on her visits, Connor received a pre-calculated hourly dose of pain medication through a PICC line (peripherally inserted central catheter) and was able to dose himself for breakthrough pain by pushing a button.

Though Connor was reluctant to admit this additional mechanical device into his life, he was grateful to have his pain relieved. The PCA allowed him to be comfortable and alert, a state he was unable to accomplish with liquid oral pain medications, and he made some trips out of the house—to church, to a barbeque given in his honor as a fundraiser for his family, and to the occasional sporting event where one or both of his boys were playing football or basketball. His quality of life improved, and he leeched enough strength from his TPN and his PCA to keep going for several more weeks. He felt so good, in fact, that he scheduled another appointment at his cancer clinic, hoping they might have something new for him to try. Connor was a nice guy, and he was young, so they did not refuse him the appointment, though they knew that they had nothing for him that would cure his cancer or give him any more sustainable quality of life than he already had.

When Connor began to decline such that he could no longer walk safely without assistance, a series of friends came to help out so his wife could continue to work. Eventually she had to take a leave of absence and stay home herself. When he became fully confined to the recliner, no longer able to get up even with assistance, they reluctantly accepted a hospital bed with automatic controls. For a while, this lent some improvement to Connor's tremendous lower body swelling that had been made worse by sitting in his chair twenty-four hours a day. The bed was set up next to the window where his recliner had been and they adjusted to another "new normal" for a while.

Eventually, Connor began to sleep much of the time and require increasing dosing of his pain medication to control his symptoms. His edema worsened and he began to be short of breath. Connor had reached a maximum benefit of living almost an additional year on TPN, but it had begun to work against him; he was not absorbing enough nutrients to feel well, and his body was no longer able to process the intravenous fluid. He began to collect fluid under his skin—in his feet, his legs, and his belly. Eventually even his arms and hands would swell, and his lungs became congested, giving him a chronic cough and the need for supplemental oxygen. Connor's hospice nurse had discussed many times with him and his wife that there would be a time when the TPN should stop, because a body that is over-loaded with fluid has a terrible time letting go.

The dying process of an aggressively artificially hydrated body is a scene of chaotic suffering and helplessness; there is no medical procedure to remove excess fluid from the lungs when the kidneys are no longer functional enough to respond to the medications known to persuade them to dump the excess fluid, and the patient experiences a drowning that cannot be relieved other than by heavy sedation. To witness a loved one gasping for air and gurgling with fluid that comes up out of the airway is a devastating experience. Mechanical suctioning cannot keep up with the fluid production and is traumatic in itself. This is a scene that is not unfamiliar to hospice workers who inherit the care of a recently hospitalized patient whose family members *insisted* on IV hydration *with a prognosis of hours to days* because of their poorly informed opinion that no one should die of dehydration or starvation.

During the political and cultural debate over the fate of Terry Schiavo, there was much misinformation presented through the media regarding the presumptive pain associated with dehydration. Most people receive information in sensational packages that grab the attention; others have it passed on to them second hand from relatives, friends of friends, or neighbors—all of whom have an opinion of what *should* be done for someone who is dying, whether or not the opinion comes from personal experience or hearsay or any real knowledge.

In my experience with hundreds of people at the end of life, I have found that people die more comfortably and peacefully if they have been allowed to slowly decrease their oral intake, guided by their preferences and desires. There is less respiratory distress during their last hours if they have stopped eating and then stopped drinking for at least a few days. Thirst can be managed by keeping the mouth moist with swabs or ice chips or drips of water on the lips and tongue. Cracked lips need moisturizer and the mouth needs to be cleaned frequently and gently to prevent the build-up of crusted secretions; with attention to these details patients do not suffer from symptoms of terminal dehydration.

However, when someone has become dependent on artificial hydration (or nutrition) for a long time, it is very difficult to find a stopping place to say, "No more." This requires a deliberate decision, carrying the weight of finality about letting go of a life-prolonging therapy—even when it is causing suffering and threatens to cause much more if continued. Connor was in that difficult place. He was tired, and on one level ready to be done with his suffering. On another, he could not face preparing his wife and sons for the heartbreaking task of letting him go, and so lived in the conundrum of putting off the conversations he intended to have with them until he was unable to have them at all, and they were left to someone else.

What Connor was too sick to see was that everyone around him was as ready as they would ever be. His care consumed the full attention of his wife, his parents and siblings, his friends, his professional caregivers, and his children. Every aspect of each life that touched his was consumed in the love and care and impending loss of him. Everyone, including Connor, was at the wall, and his remaining conscious desire to continue to *be* transformed his living into a prolonged and protracted dying. Connor was so over-hydrated that if the TPN were stopped, he could still live off the fluid in his body for days. He agreed to slow the rate of infusion, yet he could not decide to stop it.

Knowing that if the TPN was not stopped, Connor's suffering would increase, his hospice nurse spent hours in compassionate listening and gentle persuading, to no avail. I and my hospice team prepared ourselves for a terrible death scene, which (counter to our usual recommendations) we concluded his sons ought not witness. We waited, watched, and we prayed for Connor and his family.

Two days before he died, Connor changed his mind. A peace came over him and a calm that was not dependent on the management of his physical symptoms. He was ready, and he wanted the TPN stopped. Connor died as peacefully as possible at home. His children were not present but understood that he would be dying soon. Their stepmother was doubly grieved at losing Connor and then most likely losing her close relationship with his children, who would thereafter live with their mother all the time.

Where was God in this story? When is it the right thing to step back and allow another to do what you believe to be the wrong thing? Where can we find the grace to accept that people need to find their own way, even if it means rejecting the knowledge and expertise we might offer them to ease that journey? How do we learn to listen, when what we are hearing is not what we want to hear? How do we pray for the strength to "get ready" for our own death and the going home to God, and then to act accordingly when we get what we pray for?

CHAPTER 12

Promise Me

Very truly, I tell you, when you were younger, you used to
fasten your own belt and to go wherever you wished. But
when you grow old, you will stretch out your hands, and
someone else will fasten a belt around you and take you
where you do not wish to go.

—JOHN 21:18

"I promised her I would never put her (or him) in a nursing
home." I have heard these words many times from spouses,
sons, and daughters—mostly daughters. They tell of a promise
that was made in love, and with all good intentions, and of a
promise that should never have been made, nor exacted. Each
time I have heard this line from a troubled, exhausted, and guilty
loved one, it has made me cringe, because it marked an invisible
wall between a care-weary impossible situation full of suffering
for all involved, and what could have been some relief for that
situation.

Nursing home care is generally considered to be a last resort
when all other attempts of family to care for someone at home
have failed. More often than not, the choice to seek nursing
home care becomes the burden of caregivers; few individuals
choose this option for themselves. It is natural to want to be able
to care for someone you love, even when that love is part of a
complicated relationship. It is natural to want to be cared for in

a setting that is familiar, with the right amounts of privacy and community to provide safety and security for one who is slowing down with aging or coping with a failing mind or body. However, as people's needs for care increase, a home that served a family well for a lifetime can become an obstacle course of stairs, inaccessible bathrooms, treacherous pathways through narrow doorways, and heavy furniture that has become all sharp edges and glass. Rarely, I have seen families make creative accommodations to address these issues in order to sustain a spouse or parent or grandparent in a home; many people do not have the financial resources to move to a new house, or to do a full remodel of their existing home to make room for a relative requiring supervision and care.

There can also be a resistance to making these accommodations from those who cannot imagine a change from the familiar. I have cared for patients for whom self-determination trumped all concerns for life and limb, including people in their nineties who lived alone and refused to consider allowing a higher level of care for themselves, even after spending multiple nights on the floor after falls, waiting for someone to find them the following day. This resistance becomes their undoing, when eventually one fall leads to fractures of hips or spine, and the ability to walk, or even transfer from bed to chair without assistance, is lost.

Louise was just such a resistor. She was tiny and frail and managed to live alone in her small house for several years after her husband died, depending on friends in the neighborhood for company and rides for groceries. She had never learned to drive a car, and most of the six children she had raised there had moved to distant states. She wanted her house to be intact and unchanged, just like it was when her husband was alive, and refused to replace aging carpet that had developed trip-prone ripples after being cleaned, or to repair the handrails on the front porch stairs that had begun to wobble with time.

Her dementia moved in with her so slowly that it was at first recognizable only as little quirks of aging—clipping hundreds of coupons for things she would never buy, sorting junk mail into dozens of piles, using the microwave as a breadbox because she could never learn how to use it for its intended purpose. "I don't ever want to go to a nursing home to live with a bunch of old people!" was one of Louise's mantras, and I heard it frequently because she was my mother. Being thirty-eight years younger than she was, I was never sure what she meant by "old people." She certainly did not include herself.

As her dementia progressed, my siblings and I tried to intervene in ways that seemed logical and appropriate to us—hiring a cleaning service, which she fired; scheduling more frequent visits, which she would forget about until we showed up at the door after a long drive or flight. Her letters, which had always been painstakingly handwritten on stationery, became less chatty and more cursory and threadbare. She did allow the daughter who lived the closest to her to be her power-of-attorney and to be a co-signer on her bank accounts; it was then that my sister found those telltale signs of an elder who had more money than she thought, and who had let some of it drift away to charities and other causes, oblivious of frauds or charlatans. When she quit bathing (claiming that she already had) and stopped washing her clothes, the challenges of her incontinence were all too evident, and we began to speak with her about alternative living arrangements. Because she had lived with and cared for a challenging mother-in-law in the early years of her own marriage, she swore she would never live with any of her children and she had managed to remember this self-imposed rule. When three of my siblings and I were together for the purpose of addressing her failing to perform her ADL's (activities of daily living), we managed a well-planned and poorly-executed conversation with her about our perceived need for her to be better cared for than she was. She became angry and tearful, telling us we would carry her out of her house "feet first," and "if we felt we needed to go to court to take over her life we could just try and see how far that got us!" End of conversation. In a subsequent phone call with a distant sister who could not be present for the conversation, I relayed what my mother had said, and explained that legally she had us—until something worse happened. She would have to get hurt, or lost, or do something really crazy in public (like walking down the street without her clothes) for a judge to allow us to obtain guardianship and get her admitted some-place against her will.

And then she did get hurt. She fell getting out of bed in my sister's guest room a few days after that painful encounter and broke fragile and osteoporotic bones in her lumbar spine and her pelvis. An admission to the hospital for a couple of days gave little time to scramble for a new arrangement, which wound up being an assisted living facility closer to the daughter-agent's home than her own forty-year-old house had been. We told her the move would be temporary and she believed this meant she would go home again. In fact, it *was* temporary because she was already beyond engaging in the life intended in an assisted living facility. She was beyond participation in outings and activities; she was beyond making new friends; she needed a high level of assistance for bathing and dressing and could not manage to use the remote to control her television, which became the focus of her days—always the same channel because she could not remember how to change it to another.

Assisted living facilities make a lot of promises they cannot always keep when they accept residents with high care needs. Families choose them because their appearance is for the most part more well-appointed than most nursing homes. The most lovely are the most pricey. Residents are usually able to have their own rooms or suites, and to bring in their own furnishings. These spaces are sold as little mini-apartments with dining facilities just down the hall and professional help a few steps away if needed. Add-on services of medication administration, assistance with bathing, dressing, laundry, and guidance about the facility are categorized into tiers that raise the baseline cost per month. In truth, most assisted living homes are not required to have registered nurses in house (as most nursing homes are) and frequently the "assistance" is by medical technicians or certified nursing assistants who are not trained or qualified to make judgments about whether someone is sick or requires a medication prescribed "as needed." They can hand medication to a resident when requested or on a schedule (with an added cost) but cannot "administer" it. Over the past ten to fifteen years, assisted living facilities have taken on sicker and more debilitated patients who are largely left on their own in their rooms or rolled into common areas to spend the days in their wheel chairs. They admit patients who would qualify for nursing home care, because those "promises" not to put an elderly relative in a nursing home work in their favor.[1] Assisted living facilities are invariably "for-profit" and private-pay, without any type of federal or state programs to assist residents with payment, though the cost of assisted living, at thousands of dollars per month, may still be less than private pay costs for nursing home care. Some families make the choice for assisted living for financial reasons—trying to stretch out resources for as long into a life trajectory as possible. Still other residents and their families choose assisted living because they do not want to believe that things with themselves or their loved ones are really bad enough for a nursing home yet. If a resident is moved to an assisted living facility and cannot make her own way to meals without being prompted as to the time or even the need to eat, it is likely she has missed her window for this type of living arrangement, and she will languish alone in her pretty private room while she makes everyone feel better that "at least she is not in a nursing home."

Louise declined rapidly, suffering the common infections of the failing elderly—pneumonias and urinary tract infections—and repeated trips to the hospital through the emergency room did little to help her orient to a new place and a new life. Each trip meant a new space, a new doctor, a new opinion about what was needed for her well-being until she stopped eating and it looked like she was not going to get any better. She would definitely not go home again.

---

1. Patricia McGinnis, "Assisted Living: A Crisis in Care," *Aging Today*, January/February 2014, *http://www.asaging.org/blog/assisted-living-crisis-care*; A. C. Thompson and Jonathan Jones, "The Emerald City: Life and Death in Assisted Living," *ProPublica* in collaboration with *Frontline*, July 29, 2013, *https://www.propublica.org/article/emeritus -1-the-emerald-city*.

For those who have limitless financial resources, allowing a loved one to stay in their own home with round-the-clock paid professional caregivers is one way to spend those resources, though supervising such an arrangement, even if in a geographically accessible place, carries the burdens of a thousand decisions and potential unexpected crises that inevitably arise. Aging relatives, even with dementia, continue to want to be in charge on their own turf, and do not always agree or comply with decisions made in their own best interests. This most certainly would have been the case with Louise.

It is almost as costly to bring a parent or other dependent relative into one's own home with paid caregivers to assist while at work or fulfilling other responsibilities; it saves the expense of running duplicate households and improves eyes-on supervision, yet for the time it saves going in and out of the elder's primary home, there is a larger non-monetary cost to the hosting family. Moving a parent, grandparent, or other relative with high care needs into one's home requires the effort and expense to elder-proof the environment, making accommodations around stairs, building ramps in and out of the house, or possibly remodeling wheelchair-inaccessible doorways or unusable bathrooms. When this can be accomplished, and when the one to be cared for is that lovely person who is both cheerful and grateful in her waning years and under mounting dependence on her family, this arrangement can be a wonderful thing. The image of inviting a wise elder who dispenses grace and assistance to a household of children and grandchildren, or making space in the guest room for an aging couple meant to rest in their rocking chairs after a long and happy marriage, is for some a reality to treasure. For others, this ideal gets submerged in the realities of aging and its insults that compound a history of difficult relationships and years of family dysfunction. "Getting old is not for sissies," a phrase coined by Bette Davis, could be extrapolated to include, "Caring for the old is not for sissies."

Many people feel they have no choice but to take on the personal care of their aging parents who were not able to accumulate the financial resources to pay for their own care in their declining years. Some shoulder the burden out of habit, where long-established family patterns are set—where "Mama always gets what Mama wants." Grown children can feel they have no option but to bring a declining parent into a house already bursting with adolescents or young children, even when that elder is reluctant, unpleasant, and takes over the emotional climate of the household. Sadly, in some cases families develop financial dependence upon an elder's retirement income, and the line between care and exploitation begins to blur.

These hard decisions about care are becoming more common and more necessary as our population ages overall—many are surviving diseases to which prior generations succumbed, and are living longer periods with debility and dementia than their own parents or grandparents did. As a society we have sought to extend the trajectory of our mortal lives through science and medicine with little thought as to what that might mean. Our fantasies about living to a "ripe old age" have run up against the reality of what "ripe" really means when our usefulness has faded and our need for care alters life as we know it for ourselves and those we love.

The experience of caring for an elder in the home is often kept in the family—because it can be terrible, and because there is too much guilt to speak publicly of how terrible it can be. There are losses of privacy and autonomy on all sides. Being "on duty" 24/7 as a caregiver can mean chronic loss of sleep and personal down-time; vacations can be tremendously problematic and friends go by the wayside; it makes a soul weary over time. And because the reality that is being lived was supposed to be different, and because we are supposed to be grateful and generous and loving, we are ashamed to admit how frustrating and difficult it can be, and so we isolate ourselves in our caregiving, even as our elders are isolated from the world by their need for special care.

My siblings and I chose not to bring our mother into any of our homes—because of her long and often-stated wish not to live with any of her children, and because of the considerable sacrifice it would have demanded of any of our families. Some of my siblings were already caring for aging in-laws, and were tapped out in space and energy. Because Louise had moved past being safely being cared for in her own home, because her dementia had caused her to be uncooperative with hired caregivers on her own turf, and because no one of us was close enough to her home to supervise adequately, my family grappled with what to do for our mother. My sister was understandably weary from being her sole local caretaker, so after Louise had failed her trial of assisted living, and had declined further during short-term rehab after her fractures and infections, we had her transported by private ambulance to my small town four hours away. I knew all the doctors and most of the nurses, and with my professional knowledge and experience as a family physician, I could manage her care more easily than my sister trying to negotiate decisions in a larger city with multiple providers. I secured Louise a bed in a local nursing home, asked a colleague to be her primary care physician, and began a long process of making peace with that necessary next step in her journey.

Few healthy people venture into nursing homes, unless for work or to visit someone important in their lives, and few people like what they see. Nursing homes are by and large filled with people who are old (Mom was right about that), infirm, or disabled. They are built for institutional utility, allowing the necessary feeding, bathing, changing and moving of dependent people to be done with the fewest possible workers, who by some irony are paid very low wages for such physically and emotionally difficult work. Some corporations in the nursing home business, which can be for-profit or non-profit, have upgraded their physical plants and introduced therapies that cater to the need for temporary rehabilitation after hospitalization or surgery; this type of admission pays more per patient per day than long-term or custodial care, which includes basic food, shelter and personal care typically needed for the rest of a patient's natural life. The costs of custodial care are barely covered by Medicaid when a resident is destitute and any available Social Security income they might have earned does not cover the entire bill. To get to this qualifying place for Medicaid coverage, all of an individual's assets, including cash, savings, and property, must be spent on his or her care first. It is not unusual for families to try to hide some of these assets, happy to justify shifting the cost of care to the taxpayers of their state so that what Mom and Dad "worked so hard for" could be passed on to family members instead of being used to cover the expenses of their care. With the public trust in mind, Medicaid has gotten more savvy over the years in recovering the costs of care for which they were billed. For example, if there are properties to be liquidated after the death of individuals who had received benefit from Medicaid payments for their nursing home care, Medicaid can now recover some of those monies.

Some nursing homes are better than others in appearance, some are better in the quality of their staff, and some have brought in amenities such as an activities room, or greater patient choice regarding meal options or the scheduling of their days. Most function under a burden of rules, regulations, and certifications that are intended to assure that a minimum standard of care is received by each resident. Regulations can create uniformity, but excessive regulations can stifle creativity in places of caregiving.

Fearful stories of nursing home care seem to focus on the unanswered call bell, or life in a wasteland of humanity, smelling and yelling and waiting for help in a world where privacy and dignity have been sacrificed to schedules and expediency. Yet nursing homes can also be filled with kind and generous workers who feel called to work with the dependent elderly. Though they are overworked and underpaid as a rule, many nurses and aides in nursing homes are gifted with inexplicable tenderness and manage often under great stressors to treat their charges—even when confused and combative—with dignity, respect, and love.

Louise was initially placed in a semi-private room for rehabilitation following her hospitalization, and she received physical and occupational therapies in addition to her room and board, services most often covered by Medicare for a finite number of days. A therapist eventually got her up to a walker with the goal of keeping her ambulatory. I came to see this as a dangerous idea when she continued to fall—because her dementia clouded her judgment so that she could not remember to use her walker correctly if she could remember to use it all, and because no one in a nursing home can receive fully adequate supervision around the clock. It took some doing to convince the facility administrators and the therapists that getting her used to a wheelchair was the better part of valor in this case. There is a point past which demands of even the best therapies to restore function to a failing body are unreasonable—a stress to the patient and a waste of resources.

I had requested a private room on admission and Louise was placed on a waiting list for one of the few in the facility to become available. She could afford the higher cost and was paying out of pocket from her Social Security income and her savings after her allowable rehabilitation days covered by Medicare were used up. The day her centrally located and easily viewed private room became available was the day all hell broke loose. Louise came out of a quiet and mostly cooperative shell to scream and resist being moved. She did not particularly know or like her current roommate, but she had gotten used to her surroundings and simply rebelled at having them changed again without her consent. This move coincided with an escalation of paranoia and some delusions about her "things gone missing," not an infrequent or completely unbelievable occurrence in a nursing home, and also not an infrequent symptom of progressive dementia. Nevertheless, all the accumulated changes Louise had suffered caused an explosion of emotion that lasted a few days.

A small dose of medication for her delusions helped to calm her and the move was made. I hung familiar pictures on her wall, including her favorites: the wedding pictures of all of her grown children and grandchildren and the pictures of her hot air balloon ride she had requested as an eightieth birthday present. I was able to put bird feeders outside her window and she watched them constantly, as she had for years when she lived in her own home. Eventually she adjusted to a smaller world where all her needs were met and the medication to treat her delusional behavior was withdrawn. Its only side effect was to have given her an appetite she had not had for years. She would have been mortified to realize that her weight had gone up from her usual 90 pounds to 105, causing the need to buy her some new pants. When the medication was discontinued, she slowly lost the weight back to 95 pounds or less. Early on in her tenure at the nursing home, she would like to go out for rides to see the springtime blooms or fall leaves, and I would occasionally take her to my house for a meal or to visit. One day she looked at me when we had driven only a few miles and she said she needed to get "home" soon, because they would be waiting for her. Her successful adjustment and her progressing dementia had caused a shift in her perspective about the nursing home, and a shift in her identity to someone who belonged there—who *wanted* to be there.

Louise lived five years in that nursing home, surprising me with a stamina for living one day after the other, and teaching me about the gifts that can be found in a life diminished by time and insult. I cannot say that all of her days were good days, but I can say that some of them were. I witnessed people caring for her with tenderness and with affection as well as with efficiency. I saw her smiling at visitors, using her company manners, even when she did not know who they were. I saw her singing along to old hymns I did not know she knew when the activities director played music for the residents. They told me her favorite was "I'll Fly Away," and they usually had to play and sing it twice because she would always ask for it to be played, having forgotten they had already sung it earlier in that day's program, probably earlier that same hour.

I watched her anxiety fade with her strength as she began to live from a place of gratitude for what I had judged to be a less-than-desirable existence. It was clear to me that my mother felt cared for, and though my siblings and I certainly worked through our various kinds of guilt at not being the ones to provide that care, we came to see that she had long ago made the right decision for her family. Though she had never wanted to live with "old people," she was more determined that her fading years would not become a daily imposition on her children and grandchildren. That was the final and ultimate gift that she gave her six children.

Louise began to fade in earnest after a series of aspirations that led to pneumonias. With the progression of her dementia, she forgot how to speak, and then how to use a fork and spoon, and then how to swallow. I had long before promised her she would never have to go to another hospital, and we treated her in place—avoiding the revolving door of nursing home to emergency room to hospital to nursing home—initially with oral antibiotics with some success.

Eventually her frailty outwitted the gentle interventions and she died in her room with her pictures on the wall and the birds feeding just outside her window. For her last several days, she needed little beyond the presence of those who cared for her checking in on her, ate nothing, and said little; after a day of needing a few small doses of morphine to help with her breathing, she gently let go, following at last the love of her life from whom she had been widowed and separated for fifteen long years. As we gathered as a family to say our goodbyes at her funeral, we sang "I'll Fly Away," *twice*.

Nursing homes are in our world to stay, as our American population is aging, with people who are living longer periods of debility and dependence. There will in the next generation be too many of us for too few of us to care for, and most of us will need to depend on institutional care for ourselves or our loved ones as we cope with escalating numbers of people suffering from dementia and from chronic and progressive physical illnesses. Living a long life is only very rarely managed with intact body and with mind enough to become a revered repository of wisdom for generations who follow.

How can we begin to consider these places of care as not only necessary, but important and valuable? How can we support those who live in nursing homes beyond the one annual Christmas-gift-and-caroling hour organized by well-meaning church groups or civic organizations? Where is the balance between individual autonomy and privacy and the requirements of communal living? What resources are we willing to spend on the care of our elderly—individually and collectively? Are we even willing to spend *their* resources, or do we try to hoard our own family's accumulated wealth while seeking to use taxpayer sources of funding for our elders' care? Do those who do the difficult hands-on care in nursing homes—those whom we expect to be both expertly trained and tender—receive our respect, our gratitude, and a living wage? Where is God in these waning years and all the decisions we make for those who need high levels of care? Why does God wait so long to take some people home? What is God trying to teach us about our mortality?

CHAPTER 13

Grace

Do not be envious when some become rich,
   or when the grandeur of their house increases;
For they will carry nothing away at their death,
   nor will their grandeur follow them.
Though they thought highly of themselves while they lived,
   and were praised for their success,
They shall join the company of their forebears,
   who will never see the light again.
Those who are honored, but have no understanding,
   are like the beasts that perish.

—Psalm 49:16–20 BCP

Grace was a matriarch in her Deep South hometown. It was a position she had inherited from her mother and her grandmother before her; though she had married well and taken her husband's name, her identity was deeply rooted in her own family's status and generational wealth. She was a widow in her early sixties but by no means a poor one; by all outward appearances Grace's world of privilege should have sheltered her from any conceivable adversity. She lived in a plantation style mansion built on a bluff overlooking a river. Built by her grandfather, its white columns could be seen peeking through giant magnolia trees and the low-hanging branches of live oaks dripping with Spanish moss all along the winding driveway to her front door.

The first time I approached Grace's grand front entrance I carried my faithful companions, anxiety and dread, always ready to accompany me into a home of immense privilege where someone was dying. My perceptions that people with great wealth have great expectations and are difficult to please were formed by experience. I expected that my role in this house would include long, painful conversations about what was possible and what was not possible, at any price, to reverse or arrest a terminal prognosis. People who were used to getting what they wanted were slow to understand that when it came to dying, no one got what they really wanted, which was not to die.

Grace had lived out the role of "pillar of the community" that had been expected of her. She had sat on boards of directors for several charitable organizations, was a past president of a prestigious garden club, and was known for opening her expansive home and grounds for a "tour of homes" annual fund raiser for a children's home. She had for many years hosted a fund-raising gala for the local children's hospital that involved formal attire and large checks. She knew everyone in town, and those she did not know, she could find out about from someone she did. Grace had done her research about hospice care months earlier—not about *what* all it entailed but about *who* was involved and *what* credentials they carried into her home—and she had rejected it as an option for herself thus far. I did not have much information about Grace's illness but I knew that this particular invitation had been personally transmitted through my own board president. I knew that I was stepping into a world where trust did not come easy and where the time and energy required of my hospice team would be significant.

Grace's physical decline had begun two years earlier when she stumbled walking on a cobblestone street and fell. It was easy at first to blame the old bricks, worn slick and uneven by generations of traffic, and she did. But then she began to stumble a lot, and to drop things. Her speech began to have a slight slur, and people began to wonder if Grace had a problem with alcohol. She continued to push through her busy life, not wanting to admit that something was wrong. Eventually she casually mentioned her concerns to one of her physicians at a social event; she could not bear sitting in a doctor's waiting room and he came to see her at her home. Suspecting something significantly wrong with Grace, he persuaded her to travel to larger city for a series of specialty examinations and tests.

When she received a diagnosis of ALS (Amyotrophic Lateral Sclerosis) Grace kept it to herself. There was no room in her life for a debilitating and degenerative disease without a cure. She withdrew from activities that had demanded her participation, and built a collection of excuses that made the rounds until she was quietly and effectively cut off from her highly visible former life. No longer in the society page photographs of the local paper, no longer in the receiving lines to welcome beautiful people in formal gowns and black tie to another annual event, no longer at the club for lunch or afternoon tea, Grace disappeared inside her big house and sank slowly into weakness and isolation.

The appointment to meet Grace and her daughter-in-law Meredith was coordinated to include the nurse and social worker from our team. It took some maneuvering to get our separate schedules to converge, but we made the effort to make that happen in special cases in which the urgency of unmanaged symptoms or fractious family dynamics waited for our attention, or when the patient and family desired as few separate visits as possible to interrupt their busy lives and routine.

Met at the door by a woman in a black uniform with white apron, we crossed the threshold of the great house and stepped back in time. From the marble tiled floors dressed in well-worn Persian rugs to the plaster ceilings and chandeliers, to the upholstered furniture on highly polished spindly legs, Grace's home drew me into a past I had not known except in glimpses, or from books. I was the doctor, bringing years of education, knowledge, experience, and skills to treat the discomforts of unchecked progressive terminal disease, and yet I felt like a trespasser in Grace's beautiful house. For how could such a grand and well-appointed palace be a house of sickness and suffering?

We entered Grace's bedroom, where she had been imprisoned by her illness in a high four-poster bed. She was minimally propped on pillows and sprawled in what appeared to be an uncomfortable posture, making grunting noises that sounded like distress. Meredith stood at the side of the bed, exhausted and helpless. The young and childless widow of Grace's only son John, Meredith was the closest thing Grace had to living relative. The two women shared the grief and devastation of John's death from an accident three years earlier; they had little else in common. Meredith had maintained some contact with Grace since John's death; she really felt sorry for her as well—now alone, having lost both husband and son. Though she knew she was a poor substitute for John, Meredith had moved into Grace's house about three months earlier, taking leave from her job and putting her life and a new relationship on hold to care for Grace, who had for months refused outside assistance for bathing, dressing, and feeding.

Over the months Grace had become ever more demanding of Meredith, wanting her at her side whenever she was awake. Though her role as daughter-in-law to Grace had always been challenging, Meredith saw her caregiving role as a tribute to her dead husband, something he would have done and would have appreciated her doing; in some ways it was an act of closure for Meredith. Grace had told Meredith many times that the family's wealth would go to a charitable foundation now that the only heir was gone, so it wasn't about the money.

Unable to negotiate the stairs, Grace had allowed her world to shrink to smaller and smaller areas of her grand house, adamant not to do anything that might alter its appearance. No stair chair lift on the grand stairway, no hospital bed allowed, no walker or wheelchair visible to anyone. No scruffy sweats or pajamas for Grace; for as long as she could manage it, being completely dressed and properly made up every day was essential to her. Her illness and decline were a secret in her mind, and if the outside world did not see it, and if she did not see it in the mirror, then it did not exist.

Grace had fallen several times getting in and out of her bed, which was too high off the ground for managing safe transfers; she stayed black and blue though with bones intact thus far. She had become incontinent, though she would not wear adult briefs. She had begun choking intermittently on food brought to her on a tray, and blamed it on her cook, even as the offerings became subtly and surreptitiously softer and smoother for easier swallowing. Grace's world had fallen in around her, folding into her failing body and her crumbling spirit gradually and slowly, until she was at a loss to contain it.

Meredith had been reduced to a walking zombie of anger, depression, frustration, and tears, with no life outside the demands of her dying mother-in-law. Grace resented having a daughter-in-law who could not measure up to the impossible ideal she held—not only in the unmet standards she had held for the perfect mate for her son, but for Meredith's failure to produce a grandson or to move in the circles of society so important in Grace's life. It did not take long to see that Meredith resented these impossible expectations, yet, inexplicably, she was committed for the long haul—to the bitter end. Ignoring weeks of Grace's resistance, Meredith had finally made a decision to allow hospice in to see if we could help.

After addressing the initial shock of a diagnosis of progressive neurological disease, much of its management involves the management of the body. Most people with reasonable geographic access are referred to medical specialists or multidisciplinary specialty clinics created to treat one specific type of illness, like ALS. Establishing a relationship with an ALS clinic would have helped Grace take progressive steps to support the losses that had come with the disease, at least for a while. Walkers, power wheelchairs, stair lifts, hospital-type beds, grab-bars, portable toilets, and mechanical lifts are all tools that could have assisted Grace to compensate for the losses of speaking clearly, climbing stairs, walking, sitting up straight, and transferring from one spot to another.

Specialized instruction on diet and feeding would have been offered until her ability to swallow was completely lost, and the option for a feeding tube for supplemental nutrition would have been addressed if she was considered to be maintaining a quality of life that she might choose to extend for a short while. Some ALS patients opt for portable mechanical ventilation when they lose the muscle strength to breathe, though I found this to be a rare choice in my experience.

The most valuable offering of a specialty clinic is education and supportive preparation for disease progression, so that significant decisions are less likely left to crisis moments. Grace had not availed herself of any of this assistance—not because she could not afford the care, but because going to the specialist would only have confirmed her worst fears. Her debility already caused her so much shame that she lived in constant fear of being seen by someone who knew her. Grace's alternative was to hide in her great house and to trap Meredith there with her. The two of them fumbled along, angry and distressed, figuring things out or not, and reducing their world eventually to the space that was Grace's bedroom, leaving the rest of the large house intact and untouched by ALS.

Not infrequently my most difficult task in professional hospice care was to hold myself back, to refrain from rushing in to put whatever fix I could on any messy and messed up situation I stumbled into. Early on, I saw this compulsion to set things right as a demand of compassion, and did not recognize its bulldozing effect on the victims of my well-meaning attention. Because I thought my knowledge and objectivity were more valuable than the coping of those in extreme distress, I was ready to blaze a trail through misinformation, confusion, and poor decisions to create a serene and sacred space for dying that I thought everyone deserved and that I wanted everyone to experience—even if it required some emotional bullying to get people to consider a change of perspective, or a change of sheets.

Over time, I began to see things differently; I began to recognize all the people I encountered faced loss and dying in their own way, using their physical, emotional, and financial resources in ways that were as complex as they were varied. Decisions that had come from unseen motives or necessity, made long before my involvement in a person's dying time, could be honored and blessed, even when they made no sense to me, even when they had led to what I discerned was harm rather than help. My deep impulses to make caregiving easier, to make patients more physically comfortable, to make caregiving environments more convenient, more safe, and less dark and smelly, had to be stuffed even deeper inside myself as I tried to make a way to be present with what was. I was no longer protected by the familiar environments of the medical professional—office, clinic, hospital—where patients came seeking and at least pretending to value my opinions and my direction; instead I was wandering in the wilderness, trying to find the path between the possible and the acceptable, between hope and despair.

Grace was not happy at having strangers in her bedroom. She was no longer successfully verbal enough to express her displeasure as clearly as she would have liked, but I could see it in her eyes, and hear it in her guttural wails. She could no longer advocate for herself or make decisions on aspects of her care, so after the required physical exam screening, the hospice team went downstairs with Meredith to discuss what she would have us do for her and for Grace. Meredith had been appointed Grace's health care proxy after John's death and she had Grace's advance directive in hand. She tearfully told the heartbreaking story of her weeks trapped in a home with someone who had always been in charge, but who now was someone dependent on her for everything—bathing, dressing, feeding, and even interpreting what had become Grace's minimal and slurred communication. The secrecy about her illness that Grace had demanded in order to protect herself had become the greatest burden of all, as it had cut Meredith off from friends and professional help that could have supported her. Meredith was both relieved to have hospice involved and conflicted about her betrayal of Grace's wishes—having given Grace one more reason to be disappointed in her.

When I looked at Grace's advance directive, my heart sank. She had asked for all means to sustain her life, even mechanical ventilation if necessary. She was "Full Code," meaning when she stopped breathing, if witnessed, she expected 911 to be called, and CPR begun to restart a body that had been spent. We gently explained to Meredith what this meant. Though Meredith was the agent, Grace had never discussed this document with her; therefore it was not clear what Grace had in mind when she signed it while updating her will at the urging of her attorney after the deaths of first her husband and then her son. Because Grace had shunned medical interventions as her disease progressed, no one had asked Grace or Meredith about end-of-life plans. Without a conversation with Grace about her wishes in her present circumstances, Meredith was too conflicted to understand its repercussions for Grace at that time.

I reassured Meredith that a DNR was not required for Grace to receive hospice services, and we set about scheduling a certified nursing assistant to come in for bathing and a bed change every other day, and for delivery of a hospital bed, a mechanical lift for transfers, and other equipment and supplies to make the care for Grace more practicable. I told Meredith that I did not know how long Grace would live, but that when she was no longer able to take in nourishment, then her life expectancy would be weeks and not months. The one box that Grace had not checked on her advance directive was to request artificial nutrition by feeding tube. This would have extended Grace's life through a longer period of debility and dependence, and though it made little sense that Grace had at one time desired CPR, long before she knew she would have ALS, she evidently found something about being fed by a tube surgically placed into her stomach unacceptable under any circumstances.

That patients can be accepted into hospice care with full resuscitation orders is surprising to some. It does allow people who might be ambivalent about choosing hospice services earlier in the trajectory of their decline, when they still have some quality of life, to be open to conversations about what that quality of life means for them and how best to secure it. Some patients with a terminal diagnosis of cancer, for example, might still want treatment for pneumonia, infection, or an unrelated heart attack, if reversing a temporary crisis might still give them some quality time before their cancer reaches a stage to make that unfeasible. Most hospice patients who enter end-of-life care as Full Code eventually sign a DNR request as they decline, once they have had time to develop relationships of trust with their hospice team, and have had a chance to talk about what is really important to them at the end of their life—staying out of pain, staying out of the hospital, and being at home with their families, their friends, and their pets. Patients who cling even in their last days to some illusion of being physically restored to health usually have loved ones who can see the futility and pretense of trying to resuscitate the dying, and act as their agent to make the decision to allow them a peaceful death without interference or drama.

Even though Grace's distressing symptoms of decline improved somewhat within days to weeks of hospice care, it was not clear that Meredith would be able to make this decision. She had lived for so long under the power of Grace's will, and had such a contentious relationship with her, that giving permission to forego CPR was to Meredith too much like hastening Grace's death, a concept that was complicated by the guilt of anticipated relief of having her own life back, and the loss that comes with unfinished business.

With great relief, the hospice team began to notice that with each visit to Grace, she began to soften. Blazing anger and frustration dissipated and she began to sleep unafraid. She quit fighting the aide who came to bathe her and change her clothing and bedding every day, deciding that being clean was better than being stubborn. We had engineered getting Grace into a hospital bed in a sitting room closer to a bathroom and blessed with views shaded by the magnolias and giant live oak trees, and she seemed to enjoy looking out the windows, watching the light play on birds and squirrels. Meredith contracted with a private agency to send round-the-clock private duty nursing assistants as bedside sitters, which freed her up to run the household and have some time to herself. Driving up to Grace's mansion on the hill began to feel almost routine, as the trauma encountered on the first visit was covered, over time, by the small daily blessings that come from caring well for someone who is dying.

Then one day Grace choked on a bit of soft food that she had always enjoyed and tolerated before. She was too weak to cough it out and she began to turn blue. Meredith called 911 and off she went to the hospital emergency room where she was suctioned and intubated and placed on mechanical ventilation for respiratory failure. The peace that had been created around Grace in her home was gone, replaced by lights and noise and lines and tubes, all well intentioned to save Grace's life, which is exactly what is being requested when 911 is called in such an emergency.

Unfortunately for Grace, by this time in the trajectory of her illness she was too weak to recover her lung function and too agitated to tolerate the ventilator without sedation. Unfortunately for Meredith, she was left facing an impossible choice to make, and she was on her own. Even though hospice can care for a patient in her own home with a DNR order, and more rarely cover a brief hospitalization in a "hospice bed" for the purpose of managing symptoms that cannot be managed at home, hospice cannot assume the costs and responsibility of life support in the ICU, so this type of hospital admission comes with a discharge from hospice services.

The ICU medical team caring for Grace understood the futility in her plan of care more than they understood Meredith's reluctance to give permission to withdraw her life support. They requested a palliative care consult in the hospital, and the palliative care team, who were educated and trained to care for patients and families with end-of-life decisions, spent a great deal of time with Meredith, often joined by Grace's attending physician. They gently and patiently listened to her story of life with Grace for the previous months, and empathized with the weight of her decision. They explained that it would never be medically possible for Grace to return home unless she received a permanent tracheostomy, tolerated a home ventilator, and was fed through a surgically implanted feeding tube. She might be sustained for a while with all of this technology, but she would not recover even the little quality of life she had before she came to the hospital.

After being given the time and space to deliberate and to pray, Meredith understood that her only merciful option was to withdraw life support and to let Grace go. In the end, she concentrated on who Grace was and what she knew of how she had lived her life, not on the words of an advance directive that lived in a world of hopeful recovery before ALS. The palliative team was with Meredith when the protocol for withdrawal of the ventilator was accomplished carefully, with great attention to any symptoms of anxiety or breathlessness Grace might have experienced, and she died peacefully within an hour of having the ventilator disconnected.

Meredith held her hand, cried softly and whispered words of forgiveness and gratitude and love. She had never heard those words from Grace, but she sensed them in those peaceful weeks before her hospitalization and death. Not a perfect outcome for a hospice patient, not the scenario I would have chosen for myself or for Grace and Meredith, but it was their journey, and there was some learning in it, some light, and some peace at the end.

I had never understood the story of Ruth and Naomi from the Book of Ruth until I met Grace and Meredith. I found it incomprehensible that one so young would put her own needs and desires on hold to care for her mother-in-law, even after the loved one that held them in relationship was gone. I entered their story focused on Grace, because she was my patient; yet I what I learned from their story came from Meredith, who offered a rare opportunity to look more closely, and to understand more deeply, the power of faithfulness.

Grace was not an easy person to love, though she spent her adult life and resources in activities that were designed to make her lovable. In spite of her active social life and participation in many good causes, when she became her own cause, she had no friends close enough to be allowed into her inner circle of suffering; it would have been easier for Grace to crawl through the eye of a needle than to expose her vulnerability. Meredith had nothing to gain in caring for Grace, and in many ways she exposed herself to abuse to do so. What Meredith did have was character, and compassion, and the strength of will to, at least for a time, put another's needs above her own. In my mind Meredith represented many selfless caregivers I had met through my role as physician; even in her frustration and confusion, she was my teacher in the school of loving one another. Blessed are the meek, for they will inherit the earth. Blessed are the merciful, for they shall be shown mercy. Blessed are the pure in heart, for they will see God (Matt. 5:5, 7–8). Blessed are those who hang in to do the impossible for the impossible, to help the helpless, who sit in the darkness with others, for they carry the light of God.

What leads someone to cut herself off from help or sympathy for her illness or debility? Why do you believe some people withdraw like Grace did when they begin to decline? Where do we learn to take on a caregiving role with compassion? How do our cultural systems of care make caregiving harder than it might be otherwise? How do we as people of God support people like Grace and Meredith without trying to *fix* them?

CHAPTER 14

How Long Is This Going to Take?

How long, O LORD?
will you forget me forever?
　　how long will you hide your face from me?

How long shall I have perplexity in my mind,
and grief in my heart, day after day?
　　how long shall my enemy triumph over me?
　　　　　　　　　　　　　—PSALM 13:1–2 BCP

One of my most unusual hospice home visits was to a campground outside my small south Georgia town where "snowbirds," fleeing the harsh northern winters, lived for several months each year. Our town did not have much to offer in the way of entertainment, culture, or amenities, but the cost of living was much lower than it was in Florida.

Richard had made his way to my hospital emergency room a week or so earlier with a nagging cough, only to receive an unexpected diagnosis of advanced lung cancer. At that time there were no recommended treatments that would change his poor and short prognosis. I was on call for patients without a primary physician that night, so Richard became my patient. I referred him to an oncologist who offered him palliative chemotherapy and radiation, but Richard declined. I expected that Richard and Tandy, his wife of nineteen years, would make their way home for his final days. Then I discovered that their Winnebago *was* their home. They had sold their house and all they owned to buy their cozy travel trailer, believing that many years of adventures lay ahead of them. There was no home base, no family who could take them both in, and they were content to stay where they were. Over the past winters, they had created community with other travelers, all of whom were kind and supportive and became their family for the dying time. There was no room in the camper for a hospital bed, but a creative hospice team met Richard's needs as best they could in the space available.

Not long after his diagnosis, Richard's leg broke due to metastatic disease, leaving him unable to walk, bedbound, and completely dependent on others. He lost his appetite and stopped eating. He needed portable oxygen to help his shortness of breath and oral medications to control his pain. Richard was not a small man, but he had a very gentle nature and did not complain. He expressed gratitude and regret that Tandy had been dealt the burden of his care. Their relationship had managed to survive the permanent close quarters of camper living and they spoke to each other with humor and affection. To outsiders, Tandy was a little powerhouse of energy who took on the task of caring for her dying husband in most unusual circumstances without complaint. That did not mean that Richard's dying time was not hard. Things did not always go as expected. Tandy got little sleep, and even with the help of her friends in the campground, the situation became overwhelming as Richard lingered. One early morning I found Tandy sitting at the picnic table outside their camper, her head in her hands, tears rolling silently down her face. Her grief was not just that she was losing the love of her life, but that she knew that his needs had exceeded her ability to meet them. She asked, "How long is this going to take?" both a practical and a rhetorical question.

When someone you love is dying, it takes both the blink of an eye and an eternity. After many questions and expressions of distress at not being able to give Richard what he wanted, to die at the campground, Tandy agreed to try an inpatient hospice unit, located several miles away. They settled Richard in a sunny room with windows looking out onto large live oak trees, and a bed for Tandy so that she could stay as much as she wanted. Richard's leg fracture had become displaced in the camper, which had caused an escalation of his pain that could not have been managed in their tiny home, however good Tandy's intentions. She was now able to be at his bedside as his spouse and not his nurse and aide. Without the anxiety of his hands-on care, she was able to spend the time Richard had left being next to him and loving him.

One of the most frequent questions asked by the dying and their caregivers is "How long?" "How long does he have?" "How long does this take?" Sometimes these questions are asked weeks or months before death, when concerns include whether or not to try another cancer treatment, or if there is enough time for a bucket-list trip. Mostly the courage to ask this question arises when the time is short, usually in the last few days to two weeks. There seems to be a two-week window between a patient coping with the decline of an illness and what I liken to falling off a cliff. Terminal disease seems to creep stealthily and gradually throughout a body until it begins to overwhelm one or more major organ systems, and then there seems to be a crash. This turn in the road is marked by a patient's loss of the ability to walk, or the desire to eat. It can be signaled by an emotional disengagement with what is happening outside a rapidly shrinking personal sphere. The red flag is the need or desire to spend most of the time in bed. The effort to keep on living becomes overwhelming and the sacred and holy dying time is beginning. Families protest, "Last week she was at a birthday party!" or "Two weeks ago he was driving!" or "We just got back from the beach two weeks ago!" Because both patient and family have become accustomed to the slow accommodation of debility and decline from both disease and treatment they ask, "How could this happen so quickly?" The answer comes in the form of a very simple metaphor of a slope. When the trajectory of decline in any one patient is plotted over time, the very end of the slope is short and steep. There can be dips and partial recoveries in any terminal illness, but the slope generally stays constant. The unexpected experience of what seems a sudden downturn is born of hope that there will be more time; this is true even for those whose prognosis has exceeded expectations.

After this shift to the sacred dying time, for one who has chosen to forgo further life-sustaining treatment and hospitalizations and to spend the remaining time at home, everything changes at once. Quite often this radical shift in condition and perception prompts a patient or family to accept the hospice care that had been declined previously because it was equated with "giving up." Suddenly a whole new plan of care focused on comfort needs to be quickly accepted and learned. Patients and their caregivers who have been making decisions on their own now have an entire team of people to help, and this can be overwhelming at first. Inevitably furniture needs rearranging, a make-shift bedroom with a hospital bed is often required in a dining room or den to avoid isolating the dying one to a bedroom up an impassible staircase. Unfamiliar equipment is delivered and NO SMOKING signs are required on the doors to warn that there is oxygen in the home. Relatives need to be called so they can begin making travel arrangements around their work schedules and child-care needs. Word that "they've called in hospice" spreads, and neighbors and friends come out of the woodwork—some to be helpful, and some bringing their own drama.

When hospice first becomes involved, there is an upfront drain on the family's time as they meet their nurse, social worker, and chaplain; sometimes even a hospice doctor will visit within a short specified period of time to assess needs and assist with a plan of care. Primary caregivers, most often spouses, are usually advised to take off from work, and close family members are encouraged to provide respite as they are able if primary caregivers will allow. Close friends who are truly useful—the kind who do dishes and laundry and clean bathrooms without being asked—are helpful; the time for visits from well-meaning acquaintances is past. Some tricks to enforce this are to change the answering machine on the phone, or have it forwarded to a friend or relative; put a kind "no visitors" sign on the door; put a cooler with ice on the front porch for any food that is dropped off. If anyone is offended by these barriers, it is unlikely they have ever experienced an impending death in their family and don't understand.

Once equipment and medications are delivered and the designated caregivers know how to use them, once the caregivers have been taught safe transfers of the patient from bed to chair, bathing and turning and pulling up in the bed, and once the chaos of the transition begins to dissipate, the space can truly be made sacred, and here is how: If the patient has been accustomed to television in the background all his life, leave it on; if not, turn it off. Look for some favorite music that the dying one has always liked. Dig out old photographs and tell old stories. If it hasn't been already done, visit the funeral home and make most of the desired arrangements; it can be much more difficult to make decisions after the death. Spend time in silence and in prayer. Speak softly and tenderly to each other, not just to the patient. Say what you need to say when your heart tells you to say it. Express gratitude. Offer forgiveness. Express love. Laugh. Keep your sense of humor. Let the tears come when they will; they have a cleansing power that brings healing even in loss. This is all important while the dying one is still conscious and aware, and may want to say things, too.

Let emotion be what it is, as each person losing a loved one will express their pain differently. Do not hide your sadness from the dying one, for who would want to think no one is going to miss them? Do not hide your sadness from children; if they are kept away from this sacred time and not told about the impending death for fear of upsetting them, they will not be spared their grief, and will not have had the opportunity to prepare themselves. They will not appreciate being kept in the dark, and will learn not to trust what people tell them. It is all right for children to see adults crying and upset, as long as it is explained to them as an honest expression of sadness that the children did not cause. It is important to tell young children that the impending death does not mean that anyone else will die. They need reassurance from those who will continue to love and care for them. Some children will stay close and try to care for everyone. Some will express sadness and then a short time later want to play with friends or watch a favorite television program. Both of those behaviors are appropriate. Try to let children be who they are and not expect them to be small adults. It is fine for someone to take children away from the house to participate in activities, even while a loved one is dying, as long as it is not done to keep adults from witnessing the sadness of children. Children are the greatest sign that life continues with all of its demands and noise and silliness and needs for keeping going, but they deserve to be sad, too. And they deserve to be comforted in the way that meets their needs.

Later in the process, closer to the end, there may be days when the dying one is unresponsive to voice or touch, either as part of the disease process or as a side effect of the medications required to control pain or restlessness. This, too, can be sacred time, when life continues all around the dying one. Always trust that the dying one can hear what is being said; it is thought that hearing is the last sense to go. If emotions boil over into arguments and harsh words, take them outside and try to reconcile for the sake of the one who is loved in common. Sit at the bedside, doze off if you need to. Sing if you feel like it. Consider that each family member might need some private time with the dying one for goodbyes; give each other space.

When all of the above is said and done, and the dying time drags on, the questions will begin again: "How long can someone go without eating and drinking?" (Believe it or not, two weeks is not uncommon.) "How long does this take?" It takes as long as it takes, for the dying one to soak up all the love in that sacred space, to prepare for what comes after, sometimes to wrestle with the angels like Jacob, waiting to be blessed. Sometimes the dying one, after several days of peaceful rest, will become agitated, making non-verbal sounds and moving in the bed, as if trying to break free of something. This terminal agitation is metabolic, but I believe it is also spiritual, and usually precedes a peaceful letting go. The time it takes to the last breath is usually the time needed for each particular patient, for each particular family. I have often witnessed an explicable hanging on until a loved one arrives from a long distance to say goodbye, precipitating the last breath. I have known dying patients, the focus of long attentive vigils, to wait until everyone has left the bedside to let go. No matter how many days a family has kept vigil waiting for that last breath and whispering words of permission to let go, no matter how long the pauses have been between breaths in the previous hour, holding the space for the last breath of another person is holy and powerful. The release of a loved one is met with the release of tears as the thin veil between our reality and the next is opened for a moment, and the overwhelming presence of the Spirit of God settles on those who are left with their grief.

"How long does this take?" At the end for Tandy, it seemed like the blink of an eye. She was at Richard's side, holding his hand and praying for his release as he slipped away. Her camping friends were close by to take her back to their camper when she was ready. With the assistance of the hospice chaplain, Tandy had already made arrangements for Richard to be cremated; she intended to take his ashes home to New Jersey where she was considering moving in with a daughter temporarily as she sorted out her life without her husband. Richard's death took long enough for Tandy to forgive herself for not being able to care for him herself, for her daughter to make arrangements to travel south to help her drive the camper back up north and to take her into her home, and for Tandy to learn to know and trust the caring support staff at the inpatient hospice unit to help her through the sacred dying time.

How long, O Lord, how long? It takes as long as it takes. Can we ever be truly ready? Is it possible to control the process for the perfect letting go? Or is our task to open ourselves up to how God might work in us and through us in the sacred space of dying? How can we bring our faith to the dying time of others, to the wonder and the mystery woven through the stress and the grief? Can thinking about our own death enable us to shepherd others in theirs?

CHAPTER 15

Hazelnut Coffee

But I am like a green olive tree in the house of God;
I trust in the mercy of God for ever and ever.

—Psalm 52:8 BCP

During the years when my children were very young, time off was precious and rare, and scheduled with care around school holidays and the university calendar. Freedom from work responsibilities could not be scheduled at will or whim, but had to be negotiated with call partners; the price of being away was exacted by doubling or tripling one's work load at other times to care for their patients in turn. Before the evolution of hospital medicine to include the hospitalist specialist who is always present "in house" to care for the sickest patients, the tether between a small town physician and her professional obligations was short; release for a vacation was an act of subterfuge that one kept quiet about so as not to jinx it. Patients always seemed to know when a vacation was coming up and managed to conjure up a crisis or two at the last minute to keep me from leaving, or at least to make me feel guilty about it. It always took a couple of days away to even begin to relax and let go the weight of worry I carried for other people. It was a bit like taking off in the car in a cold, dark, thirty-degree northern morning and arriving in a sixty-degree, bright and breezy southern afternoon in March, needing to shed layers of jackets and sweaters, and not yet quite trusting the surreal change to warmth and light.

With vacation time at a premium, we used the bulk of it to visit family and friends. The holidays were parsed between siblings, parents, grandparents, aunts, uncles, and cousins, though there were occasional spring breaks spent camping or sharing a beach house with old friends who had children of similar ages. Intense togetherness on vacation can be both blessing and curse, and as captured in photographs and old stories, bonds and seals relationships for a lifetime. The stress and cost of traveling fade as memories form around new adventures added to a lifetime of stories and inside family jokes. This was never truer than when we spent time with Dave.

Dave was the cousin I loved the most, and we weren't even technically related. He had married my uncle's daughter Clara, who was several years older than I was, and his place in a sprawling extended family could not have been more secured by blood. Clara had always been kind and attentive to me from childhood, and it only made sense that she would find and marry someone like Dave. He was quick-witted, generous to a fault, and loved to play practical jokes. Dave liked cooking barbeque for a crowd, fishing, music, volleyball, and the beach, and over the years had become the soul of hospitality for all of us. Wherever we got together, usually in a large rented beach house, his was the first face we would see at the door, pulling us in, and offering a "cold drink" before we could put down the car keys.

Dave always made us feel like he had been *really* waiting for us, and that we were the best thing that had happened to him all day. Every morning, after Dave had returned from a mission to find freshly-made donuts even before the sun had come up, we would wake up to the sound of his coffee grinder grinding fresh beans for hazelnut coffee—intended primarily for my husband, the coffee-lover. The two of them would then gather the fishing poles and head out with high hopes of catching our dinner.

Dave was an early computer geek, and worked for some of the first giants of the industry before going into business for himself. I hired him to set up computers and software for my solo medical practice, and my staff had grown to know him and love him like family, too. He was the one who patiently taught me terms like "reboot." Dave was the guy with infinite patience (whose like I have not known since) for people who did not have the right kind of brains to "get" computers. He was kind while explaining things over and over, and I never saw him lose his temper.

And Dave was the kind of Christian I want to be when I grow up. One of his favorite things to do was to spend a weekend in the kitchen of an old campground cooking for those on a spiritual retreat to deepen their faith and their relationship with God. The guys in his kitchen crew were his brothers in the Spirit, and he met them weekly on Saturday mornings for breakfast and fellowship in a coffee shop close to his home. Dave was Dave—at home, at work, and on weekends, and at church. He was an authentic human being who tried to take care of everyone around him, sometimes at the cost of taking care of himself.

One Thanksgiving weekend, three generations of city relatives did the traveling to visit us small-town relatives. We hosted around fifteen people, including Dave and his family. Our accommodations included a variety of air mattresses and a competition for hot water, but it was a good-natured bunch and we had a good time.

When all had been fed in appropriate Thanksgiving fashion and had watched enough football, we packed some turkey sandwiches and took a day trip to Cumberland Island on the Georgia coast, riding the ferry over for a warm and breezy day of walking and shelling, eating gorp, and catching a ride in the back of a pickup truck belonging to a friend who worked and lived at the island's only inn. The pinnacle of the weekend, however, was not achieved until we were back at our house, and ventured downtown for the annual Christmas parade. Although this was (almost) the last year of the twentieth century, we were still all stunned to see float after float, lit up in the dark, depicting the apocalyptic end times, complete with monster-like devils. Y2K notwithstanding, it was the strangest rendition of Christmas I had ever seen, and it put us all in hysterics. I remember being afraid of offending someone local standing nearby in the dark, who might happen to come to my medical practice or to teach one of my children, while I tried unsuccessfully to shush my nieces and cousins—especially Dave. They were all wondering out loud what planet we had landed on. I can remember laughing so hard that I couldn't breathe, and of course it was worse because we were trying so hard not to laugh. That was life with Dave.

That Thanksgiving with my house full of family was great fun, and was to become more important than any of us knew. When Dave and Clara got home they each came down with a cold, and then each in turn got pneumonia. Dave did not improve at home and was hospitalized, during which time a large lump was found just above his collarbone. It was melanoma, come back many years after having a mole removed from his shoulder. He had surgery to remove the new mass after New Year's, and suffered the complication of a pulmonary embolus.

By the time he had recovered some from that, within a month's time, the melanoma had spread aggressively, invading his lungs.

The treatment available at the time was not effective, and in spite of a positive attitude, a great medical team, and a deep and abiding Christian faith that he wore like his comfortable old Georgia Tech sweatshirt, Dave began to die. He spent the last weeks of his life intentionally getting in touch with friends, near and far, to say goodbye. He made his own funeral arrangements with a former computer software customer and joked with her about his worry that "she would see him naked." Even when he became too weak to get up without help, he was offering that "cold drink" to anyone who came to see him.

When Dave began to die in earnest, I traveled on short notice to see him, knowing it would be the last visit. He had only recently been admitted to a hospice program and I could see on my arrival that his symptoms were not yet under control. A hospital bed had been delivered and set up next to the bed to which he was now confined, but he resisted making the transfer. His sister—his only sibling—was visiting. Dave was sitting up and leaning forward on a double bed; lying down increased his shortness of breath and subsequent anxiety. He was responsive enough to acknowledge when someone was in the room but was no longer conversational. He could not take anything by mouth because of his difficulty breathing.

As a physician who had some experience and training in caring for dying patients, I was angry and disappointed in his care. Dave was suffering in that way we all fear when we think about death; he was actively dying and his breathlessness was an unnecessary part of the process. I persuaded Clara and Dave's son Pete to call the hospice nurse on call to demand an urgent visit. A nurse had come earlier in the day and obtained an order for something that had not been delivered—they did not know what—and the instructions for the use of the morphine that had been provided were fuzzy to them. I cracked open the seal and gave him a dose, reassuring them, just as I had many others, that it would help and not harm him. Slowly Dave began to relax some, but still would not get into the hospital bed even with the back cranked all the way up. Everyone took turns in thirty-minute shifts sitting cross-legged behind him on the bed and holding him up in a sitting position, taking his weight so he could relax while upright. Eventually the "new" medication arrived as a trans-dermal lotion to be applied to the skin of his arm to help with anxiety, agitation, and the breathlessness, too. We used it as often as allowed, and after an hour or two he began to calm enough that we could get him into the hospital bed, with the back cranked as far up as possible. His sister went home, and it seemed he would actually rest for a while. Dave's daughter Beth went to feed her dogs at her house about ten miles away. I went into the kitchen to help with getting dinner prepared and with dishes, which had always been Dave's job at a family gathering.

After we had eaten and lingered at the table over coffee and "Dave" stories, someone came into the kitchen to get me; something had changed and Dave was breathing differently. I went back into his room to find Clara and Pete by his bed. The room was quiet, with low light. They were speaking softly to him— words of love and gratitude and release—as he was letting go. I told them it would not be long, and we called Beth, who had not returned from the dog errand, and told her to pull over to the side of the road. She stayed on the phone long enough to tell him goodbye, and then he was gone.

I had been at the bedside for many deaths before this one, but this was different. My family's style, established long ago by grandparents, was low drama; there was no wailing or acting out. Yet in their quiet tearful acceptance of what had happened to shake their worlds, I knew the depth of anguish that flooded my family; I knew the depth of their loss. I knew that the one who had not been physically present as Dave breathed his last breath would live in a sea of regret for a long time. Later, as Dave's friend the undertaker wrapped his body in a quilt and carried him out of the house, the repeat of his quip about being seen naked made us laugh, but did not prevent my perception that Clara was leaving too, going to a place of devastation that would turn her to stone right in front of me, a place I could not follow to console her.

At Dave's funeral, I know the music was tender and the flowers were beautiful, though I scarcely remember them. What I do remember is that seven different men who asked to speak stood in front of a full church and each one said that Dave had been his best friend. I believed that was true—that if anyone could make that many people feel like he was their best friend, it was Dave.

Much later, probably months later, when we were still treading lightly around his memory in our family gatherings, I mentioned that my husband, Mark, always appreciated Dave making him that fresh cup of hazelnut coffee on those pre-dawn mornings at the beach. Though Mark had *never liked* hazelnut coffee, he would drink it gladly and gratefully because Dave enjoyed making it and serving it so much that he did not want to spoil his pleasure. Everyone in the room burst out laughing and laughed themselves to tears. I thought it was a sweet story but not *that* funny, until they were able to tell me that Dave *never liked hazelnut coffee either*, and just kept making it because he thought Mark liked it.

Grief is a noun—something large and terrible. It can be witnessed. It can be lived. It can be manageable for some, but crippling for someone else. It can move through a life as if possessing a will of its own. It can be all-consuming and stealthy, identifiably familiar and mysteriously particular. Grief does not have a single definition, because it is a living thing that can seed and grow—in ways monstrous and beautiful—to fill the space and time that someone has left behind by death. We can recognize grief, but we cannot ever fully know the depth of its hold on another.

Grieve is a verb, the kind of word that does work, and though it is work that has a beginning, it may or may not ever be finished. We can support grieving people in this work, but we cannot do it for them. We can try to measure loss on some kind of scale that matches its intensity with a corresponding grief response, but if loss is proportional to love, what then? A life of holding back love to hold back loss would not be a life worth living.

To say that dying, the ultimate loss, is a part of living, or that we are all mortal, are statements that so embrace the obvious they have become clichés. That this makes them no less true is a conundrum with which we must wrestle—we believers in a God who loves us. Jesus was always warning his disciples that to gain the whole world meant loss was coming, and that to experience and embrace loss meant that we might glimpse eternity. Why would our God set things up so? What makes us follow such a King of Kings who in his young life turned the world as it was known upside down, all while asking his followers to be prepared to lose their lives for his sake? And if his rising again did indeed conquer death, why do we dread death so?

Would that I had the answers to all of these questions. What I do know is that all who are born will die, and most of us will lose someone we love to death before we die. And dying is not an easy business. Though we speak of it almost casually in the general—in our prayers, when we worship, when we scan the obituaries and watch the evening news—it is always unexpected, shocking even, in the particular. What I can offer to those who are staring down the coming of death, is the certainty that the dying time is somehow manageable, that there are capable and caring professionals able and willing to help in the process, that God is always present when it happens, and that when it is done thoughtfully and courageously and lovingly, it is never as scary as one might imagine. And by some inexplicable and unbidden grace, loss is survivable.

I can also testify that being a witness to dying has been its own blessing, and that the stories I carry of that witness have made me love life—fiercely and gratefully. Of this I am reminded every time I see sunlight dancing in the trees, or snow quietly falling outside a window, feel the heat in a late September afternoon, taste pound cake with a hint of bourbon, or catch the smell of hazelnut coffee.